THE VULTURE AND THE BULL

Religious Responses to Death

Antonio R. Gualtieri

UNIVERSITY
PRESS OF
AMERICA

LANHAM • NEW YORK • LONDON

Copyright © **1984 by**

University Press of America, ™ **Inc.**

4720 Boston Way
Lanham, MD 20706

3 Henrietta Street
London WC2E 8LU England

Library of Congress Cataloging in
Publication Data

Gualtieri, Antonio R., 1931–
  The Vulture and the Bull.

  Includes index.
  1. Death--Religious aspects. 2.
Future life. I. Title.
BL504.G79   1984   291.2'3   84-5247
ISBN 0-8191-3963-7 (alk. paper)
ISBN 0-8191-3964-5 (pbk.:alk.paper)

All University Press of America books are produced on acid-free
paper which exceeds the minimum standards set by the National
Historical Publications and Records Commission.

To Our Children
Julia, Joanna, Mark, Sarah

My Theological Tutors Unawares

ACKNOWLEDGEMENTS

I would like to acknowledge my gratitude to the editors of ARC (McGill University) for permission to reprint "Existential Despair or Serene Acceptance? A Note on Attitudes Towards Death." from vol. ix, No. 2 and to Abingdon Press, Nashville for permission to quote from Liston O. Mills, ed., <u>Perspectives on Death</u>; Oxford University Press for permission to quote from Gunther Zuntz, <u>Persephone: Three essays on Religion and Thought in Magna Graecia</u>; to George Allen and Unwin for permission to quote from Edward Conze, <u>Buddhist Meditation</u>.

The divine reality which dominated the minds of these people and which they worshipped in their small shrines was -- the very fact of life and death; these felt as the deeds of ruthless and unaccountable powers; death pictured in the shape of enormous vultures over headless (that is, dead) human bodies; opposing them, the goddess appears in one, ever-resurring shape, namely, in the act of giving birth. Her progeny is the bull, the essential begetter. His emblem, large actual bucrania, is everywhere, in astounding numbers, asserting his power to overcome death... The begetter and the parturient: these two are constantly undoing the work of the vultures -- whose prey is the perishable flesh ....

Gunther Zuntz, <u>Persephone</u>:
<u>Three Essays On Religion and</u>
<u>Thought In Magna Graecia</u> (14)

The toughest competition in Life is death.

Evel Knievel

CONTENTS

PREFACE

This book is an outgrowth of university courses I have taught on the meaning of death and afterlife. I am appalled in retrospect at how recent is the wide-scale introduction of such courses, an introduction prompted largely by market responses to the fashionable discussion about death in popular, often secular, circles.

If the interpretation of religion underlying this book (and to some extent exposited in it) is correct, then attention to the way in which religious traditions deal with human finitude and mortality should have been in the forefront of religious studies. My understanding of human religiousness and, derivatively, of the appropriate orientation in religious studies, is heavily influenced by Wilfred Cantwell Smith, most notably in his books The Meaning And End of Religion and the disarmingly modest but methodologically significant The Faith of Other Men.

The bibliography lists some of the works in which I have sought to elaborate the perspective on religion and religiology that animates this present enquiry into death. The definition of religion with which I operate may be briefly summarized as human participation in an historical tradition (or symbol system) in such a committed way that its implicit world and value view generates and expresses the existential selfhood or personal faith of the participants. When I am in full rhetorical flight the language I use for this religious world-and-value view is "encoded cosmological and axiological premises which entail existential paradigms." Whereas my referent for the word 'paradigm' is usually the models for living that can be extrapolated from an understanding of reality, I detect the prevailing fashion is to use 'paradigm' as does Thomas Kuhn in The Structure of Scientific Revolutions (1970: 175) to "stand for the entire constellation of beliefs, values, techniques, and so on shared by the members of a given community." This sense of 'paradigm' comes very close to my 'cosmology and axiology'. What matters, of course, is meanings, not the variable terms in which they may be expressed.

A corollary of the view of religion advocated here is that religious activity in its various forms is fundamentally an attempt to deal in a transformative, salvific way with the assaults on human wholeness and happiness by meaninglessness, guilt and death. The new self, brought into being by the internalization of the sacred knowledge encoded in religious symbols, transcends the plight of ordinary existence.

All this should have been evident to Western scholars operating out of a culture whose dominant religious tradition -- at least until recent times -- urgently reiterated its intention to rescue humankind from the twin scourges of sin and death. As I shall show, however, this negative assessment of death is characteristic of all the great religious traditions, all of which resolve to deliver their devotees from the terror and bafflement of mortality -- albeit by different soteriological strategies.

This approach is detailed in the first chapter which interprets death as pain and problem, and is introduced here only to forestall the charge that the contemporary literary preoccupation with death is a fad and, perhaps, a declining one. I cannot foresee that any serious study of religion, operating with an adequate comprehension of the nature and function of religions traditions, can abandon a sustained analysis of how religious have explained death to their devotees and proffered them a means of coping with the suffering and perplexity evoked by death.

I wish to anticipate a further objection: granted the centrality of death to religious intentions (and to any serious consideration of the human enterprise), is yet another book on the theme required? Are we not inundated with a plethora of books on death? The direct answer is that this present study deals with its material in a way sufficiently different way from existing books known to me to justify sending it forth. I have, in my teaching, used texts expositing the interpretation of death in Eastern thought or, alternatively, in Christian and Jewish thought. But few provided a more or less comprehensive survey of the history of religions, including the emergent 'religious' tradition of modernity. Where extant surveys dealt with a commendable range of materials from the history of religions, the exposition was not carried out consistenly within an adequate conceptual framework for religious studies. Increasingly there are books that concentrate on contemporary parapsychological or spiritualist phenomena but have no grounding in classical world religions.

In the halcyon days of the rapid expansion of religion departments during the sixties, the ready availability of funds permitted the engagement of specialists, concentrating on particular fields. As a consequence, the synthesizing vision in religious studies was frequently lost. There is, I believe, value in thematic studies such as the present one on death and afterlife that adopt a synoptic perspective allowing us to see both the diversity of answers given by the various traditions to common human questions, and the possibility of a persuasive consensus respecting some, at least, of these solutions.

Inasmuch as many, perhaps most, present day scholars operate with a wide definition of religion that encompasses secular systems of belief and practice that induce and express the selfhood of their adherents in a way analogous to that of customary religious traditions, I have also included the meaning of death conveyed by some atheistic schools of existentialism and naturalism.

Finally, I have come to some judgements of my own regarding the intentions and achievements of religious traditions in analysing and conquering death. I trust these insights and interpretations will be of personal as well as scholarly interest.

I want to record my thanks to Dolores Stephen who typed some of the early drafts, and Kathryne Van Zanten and Darlene Zaremba, who produced the final version. My wife, Peggy, did the drawings of elements in the Mother-Goddess tradition, including the vulture and the bull which symbolize the threat of death and the triumph of life. Additionally, she proofread and percipiently corrected my text at various stages of composition. I am grateful for her various contributions, including preparation of the index, that made this book possible.

Ottawa
February, 1984   ARG

REFERENCES

Gualtieri, Antonio Roberto
    1967 "What is Comparative Religion Comparing? The
         Subject Matter of 'Religious' Studies."
         Journal for The Scientific Study of Religion
         Vol. VI No. 1, April: 31-39.

    1969 "Faith, Tradition and Transcendence: A Study
         of Wilfred Cantwell Smith." Canadian Journal
         of Theology Vol. XV No. 2, April: 102-111.

    1978 "Are Departments of Religion Expendable?
         (Or, Once More Unto The Definition)." The
         Council on The Study of Religion Bulletin
         December: 131-132.

    1979 "Normative and Descriptive in The Study of
         Religion." Journal of Dharma Vol. IV No. 1,
         Jan-March: 8-21.

Kuhn, Thomas S.
    1970 The Structure of Scientific Revolutions.
         Chicago: University of Chicago Press.

Smith, Wilfred Cantwell
    1962 The Faith of Other Men. Toronto: Canadian
         Broadcasting Corporation. Expanded version
         New York: New American Library, 1963; New
         York: Harper & Row Torchbook, 1972.

    1963 The Meaning and End of Religion: A New
         Approach To The Religious Traditions of
         Mankind. New York: Macmillan.

CHAPTER ONE

DEATH AS PAIN AND PROBLEM

This enquiry explores the meaning of death and afterlife in selected religious traditions and secular philosophies. It is structured on the premise that death is an existential threat to which the symbol systems of religion attempt to give, in varying ways, a transformative or therapeutic answer. This somewhat prepossessing statement will become more lucid as we proceed.

I begin by examining the first, most controversial, part of the premise, namely, that death is experienced as pain and problem. To put it more starkly, death is, in some sense, experienced as unnatural, as a source of hostility against the human enterprise and its happiness. This is not to say that people are so deluded as to think they will not die; if natural means 'inevitable', then, of course, death is a natural event. But if natural means something else -- if it denotes a quality lacking absurdity or contradiction of our highest yearnings -- then death is not natural. That is the paradox. People do know that death is natural in one sense -- that it is universal and inescapable; nevertheless, death is experienced as unnatural, as a contradictory, painful and problematic element in human life. Death generates a general condition of anxiety in human consciousness.

There will undoubtedly be some who do not concur with this assumption; who claim not to fear death. They are not agitated by distress about their mortality or their finitude. If, in fact, a large number of people felt this way, it would invalidate my beginning point that death normally -- except in cases of neurosis -- is a source of despair for human beings. I hasten to add that this premise is neither gratuitous nor arbitrary.

There are at least two sources of corroborative evidence for the judgement that death is universally experienced as threat. First there is what we might call existential analysis, or what some have called philosophical anthropology. These terms refer to a kind of reflection upon the human condition that abstracts from it some sense of its manner of operation -- an understanding of how we function as human beings. The second ground for our starting point that death is normally experienced as pain and problem is the history of religions. The burden of this exploration will fall on the history of religions and not on empirical analyses of death. We shall examine various religious traditions and see how they have pronounced themselves on the question of death and the meaning of afterlife. To anticipate: the history of religions will provide ample reinforcement of the premise that death is normally experienced as a source of suffering and perplexity.

1. Existential Analysis

Having given an indication of the main sources of evidence that support our orientation, we proceed to examine the findings of existential analysis or philosophic anthropology. 'Anthropology' simply means the study of human beings. 'Philosophical' qualifies knowledge attained without the aid of revelation but simply by critical reflection upon the public data of experience in seeking to understand human existence. I begin by directing attention to Paul Tillich and particularly to his profound and influential book The Courage To Be in which he schematized the human condition. He did so in terms of a basic conflict between what he called being and non-being. But those are highly abstract terms, so let us proceed to flesh out what he meant by non-being. By non-being -- the power that is pitted against the wholeness and happiness of the human enterprise -- he meant, first of all, the threat of emptiness and meaninglessness. In the second place, he meant the threat of guilt and condemnation. And, finally, non-being signifies the threat of fate and death. Obviously, it is the third condition which we need to explore in greatest detail, but we should note, ever so briefly, what the others are. This is necessary not only for completeness, but because these fundamental human anxieties are ultimately interrelated.

The threat of meaninglessness induces the anxiety that there is no order or pattern in the universe. Accordingly, it makes no difference what one chooses to do because there is no structure to the universe or slant to reality, such as would make one course of action preferable to another. In other words, life is simply, as we say, one damn thing after another, with no particular significance to one event over another. No particular value is preferred or striven for because there is no basic skewing to reality that would imply such a value and validate a life lived in conformity with it. The universe is capricious, arbitrary, and, consequently, one course of action is as satisfactory as another. That is an intolerable state of affairs, argues Tillich. Confrontation with the apprehension that the world is not a cosmos, that is, that it possesses no underlying pattern or order evokes the sense of emptiness. A rudderless life, a life lived without purpose because we can discover no worthy aim to which we could rightly conform ourselves, generates a distressing sense of meaninglessness.

Tillich further says that we are assaulted by the threat and anxiety of guilt and condemnation. Guilt does not, in this context, mean only the sense that a personal supreme being stands in judgement upon our moral failures. It need not necessarily be a sense of rejection by a morally righteous God who weighs us in the balance, and finds that our evil deeds outweigh our good deeds. It can also mean self-judgement growing out of the experience that one has been given one's life as a gift, and that one has done little or nothing with it. The years with their opportunities pass us by and we have nothing to show that could bestow a sense of self-esteem and satisfaction. Such guilt is a self-generated condemnation resulting from a sense of failure and self-loathing. A common element that emerges in the analysis of a Canadian Broadcasting Corporation film Why Men Rape is a low self-esteem characteristic of rapists, a sense of personal unworth that is projected out upon women and which results in their victimization. This is an extreme illustration of the condition with which everyone is at one time or another confronted; the sense that one does not have any worth and is rightly condemned.

The third human threat Tillich isolated is the threat of fate and death. This, of course, is what especially interests us. The threat of fate and death means the experience of being assaulted by powers outside our control. In our Promethean moments we fondly like to suppose that we are the captain of our soul and the master of our fate. But at one time or another, we are disturbed by the consciousness that we are so easily victimized by forces about which we can do nothing. This vulnerability culminates in the experience of death. Death is the ultimate expression of fate; death is the final demonstration that there are things we cannot always control in our own interest.

Everyone, I suppose, lives with certain autobiographical images that serve to dramatize a philosophical point. Insight into the reality of fate and death came to me with great intensity in certain events of many years ago. It was in 1952, at Rivers, Manitoba when I was a student chaplain at a military parachute jumping station. Those were days which would be unintelligible to most young people today who live psychologically as well as chronologically in the period after Salk and Sabin, that is to say, after the discovery of polio vaccines. Accordingly, most would have difficulty empathizing with the anxieties of a time before a simple innoculation gave protection against the ravages of a mysterious and dreaded disease. Our base was struck by a first case of polio, and then another, and another. The first person died, followed soon by a second death. Suddenly, people began to be gravely alarmed. What had seemed something remote, namely, their mortality, came home abruptly and trenchantly. The base was quarantined; one could not move in or out of the station. Every morning when the young officers came down to the mess for their breakfast, they could be seen craning their necks and working their heads from side to side. One of the first symptoms of bulbar polio is stiffness in the neck, and by this anxious exercising of the neck they sought assurance that they had escaped the scourge for one further day. This epidemic brought home to me how human existence is enacted against a background of fate and death. Most of the people there had ambitions and dreams: of becoming a first class pilot, getting a European posting, marrying and have children or rising to the top of the hierarchy, and so on. Almost overnight, they became sensitive to the vulnerability of all those aspirations. A bug penetrated your system and that could mean the end of all expectations and hopes.

Tillich's thesis is that simply to live is to be confronted by the threat of fate and death. That is what is meant by characterizing these anxieties as existential anxieties. The word 'existential' is a complex word; like the words 'socialism' and 'mysticism', it can be ambiguous because such a diversity of meanings attach to it. Let me clarify the particular meanings I have in mind.

By 'existential' I mean, in the first place,

universal human conditions, conditions that are inescapable, in principle, in virtue of being human. Some commentators distinguish existential anxieties from neurotic anxieties. Neuroses are individual afflictions and may be only a passing thing; they may be cured by psychotherapy. To call a particular state of consciousness an existential anxiety rather than a neurotic one is to assert that the sentiment in question is an intrinsic and unavoidable part of living. To be human is to experience the particular condition about which one speaks.

The second meaning of 'existential' for our purpose is that we are dealing with conditions that are of great subjective importance. We are not dealing with trivial matters such as the colour of one's tie, or the details of the luncheon menu. To describe a concern as existential is to indicate that it is of great impact and ultimate meaning to the person.

We turn now to look briefly at another thinker who has had a profound influence not only on his professional discipline of anthropology but also upon religious studies. Clifford Geertz in a pivotal article entitled, "Religion as a Cultural System" enunciates a position which is, in some respects, strikingly similar to Paul Tillich's. Geertz says that we are, in virtue of being human, assaulted by the threat of chaos. 'Chaos' is a general term which can be assimilated to Tillich's term 'non-being'. More specifically, Geertz isolates three aspects of the threat of chaos. The first is bafflement or a sense of intellectual perplexity. The second is suffering and pain. The third is moral paradox or a sense of injustice.

By bafflement, Geertz means the prospect faced by human beings that the world may be not only uninterpreted but, in fact, uninterpretable. This is a prospect that people do not face with serenity. As a consequence they engage in a quest for lucidity; people want the world in which they live to cohere one part with another. They want it, in other words, to make sense. An arbitrary or haphazard life is ultimately psychologically intolerable; hence, persons desire models for life that correspond with the way the universe really is. To the threat that the world might not have an underlying meaning, societies respond with a resolution to discover a meaning or pattern in the world. Human beings do not sit happily or easily with the inexplicable, especially threatening events like death. Why should we have to die, or, in the event one is heroic regarding one's own personal destiny, let me put the question more pointedly. Why should our father or mother or spouse have to die? Why should we have to tolerate the cruelty of our child's death? There can scarcely be anything more painful. Why do these things happen? The intellectual perplexity elicited by such events is intolerable and cries out for resolution. Chaos must be transformed into cosmos.

The second aspect of chaos is suffering. There simply is an enormous amount of pain. There is the pain of the bodies mangled by accidents, ravaged by incurable sickness, burned and mutilated by napalm and fragmentation bombs, or debilitated by starvation. To all this physical suffering one must add the pain of loneliness, failure, bereavement, unrequited love. Dying itself usually entails suffering. Some have what Christian devotion used to call a blessed death; their death comes easily and painlessly. But many people have a dreadfully cruel time leaving this earthly frame. The presence and prospect of suffering is experienced as chaos and threat.

Chaos is constituted, in the third place, by moral paradox. This is the sense of the inequitable distribution of suffering. As if suffering were not bad enough, it is rendered even less tolerable by the absence of fit or correspondence between the deeds and character of persons and the amount of suffering they experience. This incongruence of deed and destiny is what Geertz calls moral paradox. Those familiar with Jewish or Christian scriptures should be quite at home with this idea. In the Old Testament, the Psalmist laments, "Why do the wicked flourish as the green bay tree?" It ought not to be thus; in an orderly world the wicked ought to get it in the neck and the righteous should flourish. But all too frequently we see quite the opposite. One surveys the faces of emaciated refugee children alongside the medal-bedecked chests of the juntas and has to conclude that something is wrong. The militarist adventurers seem not to suffer to any appropriate extent; more frequently the victims are the helpless non-combatants of society. This unjust and apparently irrational distribution of human pain poses an even greater problem for human understanding. This is seen pre-eminently in the experience of death; if only it were the evil doers -- racists, militarists, exploiters, despots -- who died untimely deaths. Instead, the contrary seems to be predominantly the case.

Allow me to illustrate once again with an anecdote which is my paradigm for the irrationality of death. It concerns an extraordinarily talented woman who was very artistic musically and in painting, active in her community, a dedicated mother and homekeeper and, to cap it all, a happy person who gave a great deal of pleasure to whomsoever she met. While driving home from a rushed late afternoon grocery shopping she met an oncoming truck just as it hit a pothole in the deteriorated road. The truck had a badly rusted body; the jolt as it went over the pothole caused the tailgate to tear out from its mountings and go slicing through her windshield. The mother of five very young children was instantly decapitated. This story illustrates what I mean by the maldistribution of death. The wrong people seem to die, and the result is a distressing anxiety that life is inherently chaotic.

We have noted the congruence of the existential analyses of the philosophical theologian Paul Tillich and the anthropologist Clifford Geertz. The intention has been to confirm the premise with which we began, namely, that death is experienced as an existential threat, inducing so deep an anxiety as to inspire the quest for some kind of answer to the pain and problem of death. Nevertheless this remains a highly debatable and frequently challenged thesis. Accordingly, some additional argument to make it more compelling is appropriate.

Death at the proper time, that is to say, when mental and physical energies and capacities are largely spent and when the human system is at the point of natural run-down is, I concede, not especially intimidating. In fact, such a death could readily be seen as a friend. Moreover, it is also likely that the end point of the degenerative process of the organism will coincide with the discharge of important human social duties and with the attainment of valuable life experience of love and creativity. To illustrate: It used to be one of my adolescent fantasies, derived from reading mountaineering accounts, to go to Mount Everest and K2 -- the highest and second highest mountains in the world. In later years I trekked through the Himalaya and Karakoram ranges to the bases of these awesome peaks. More to the point, the passage of years brought me a spirited and talented wife and four

enjoyable and rewarding (and challenging!) children.
By the time the body starts to run down, the chances
are one has got some significant human undertakings
accomplished.

This point may be further illumined by the image
of the fulfilled householder taken from Hindu
tradition. In the fullness of years, when vision fails
and limbs grow weary, and one has seen one's first
grandson, then one is considered to have fulfilled most
domestic and communal duties and is, accordingly, free
to abandon the obligations of family and society and to
engage in the spiritual pursuit of deliverance from
this world of space/time, from the weary cycle of
rebirth. Death at such a point would not be fearsome
and most persons could likely face it with serenity,
and, in some cases, even with expectancy.

If all death occurred in the fashion described
above, my premise would be invalidated. The trickery
of death, however, is that it is not, in individual
cases, rational and just. It is not only those
advanced in years and heavy with age who die. Were
this so, the sting of death, if not removed, would at
least be assuaged. Death, however, is unpredictable,
and it is absurd. It strikes down those whose lives
are just beginning, and mocks parental love. Death
insults those at the height of their creative powers in
art, in science, and in letters. Death plucks young
mothers and fathers at the time that their presence is
most urgently needed by young lives for whom they are
responsible. It is this irrational, lunatic, immoral
character of death that evokes anxiety and even
inspires rage. If we could count on the universe
unfolding as it should, and dying only when we had at
least reached three score and ten and with a bit of
luck and grace a decade or two more, then the premise
that death is pain and perplexity would be highly
debatable. But because death comes as a thief in the
night at most inopportune times, it generates the
profound human anxiety to which religious systems seek
to give a therapeutic answer.

2. The History of Religions

Let us leave philosophical anthropology which, I
have argued, supports the thesis that death is
experienced as mocker of our noblest aspirations and
our highest yearnings for happiness, and look now at

the history of religions. The approach adopted here of concentrating on religions traditions demands that we should be aware of my presuppositions about the nature of religious symbol systems. The historical study of religions ought not to be regarded as a tedious undertaking, nor as a kind of antiquarian pursuit in which one is engaged in the study of what people quaintly believed once upon a time. It is my conviction that religious traditions are, in most cases, repositories of profound understanding of the human condition, of its plight and of methods of deliverance from this human condition experienced as gone awry.

The anthropologist Edmund Leach used information and communication theory to express his conviction that the archaic elements comprising religious traditions are really compressed vehicles of knowledge. Religious stories, symbols, images, doctrines and institutions are, in effect, coded information about the nature of reality. People who participate in a religious system have conveyed to them a perspective on the world. In other words, religious symbols are a coded cosmology. A broad theory about the world -- an understanding about the meaning and value of human beings, ultimate reality, the historical process, the physical environment -- is compressed into the esoteric symbols of religious systems.

The doctrines that we shall be examining such as resurrection of the body, immortality of the soul, and the no-self doctrine of Buddhism, represent highly compressed information about the human venture. Such doctrines and certain related visual symbols are codes by which an understanding of human existence and its destiny is conveyed to initiates. Our assignment will be to decode these symbols -- to see what possible insight they contained or were thought to contain about the human situation, particularly that of finitude and mortality.

On this view it is superficial to dismiss religious images as residues of primitive and unsophisticated modes of thought. This does not, of course, mean one has to accept interpretations of human being and the universe that are implicit in various religious images; it does mean, though, that one should understand them for what they are, namely, condensed and imaginative disclosures about the meaning of life. One may not agree with the particular content of some of the religious traditions whose meanings about death this survey seeks to decipher. Indeed, one would have a hard time agreeing with all of them because some of them, at least on the surface level, appear contradictory. It is very difficult to make certain doctrines of the immortal soul in chapter two of the Bhagavad Gita, fit coherently with the doctrine of resurrection of the body in Jewish or Christian tradition. Nevertheless, the religious traditions should be paid the minimal respect of being recognized for what they are: a grappling with the great existential problems of life and resultant therapeutic discoveries that are communicated to their adherents in a compressed or coded, symbolic way. We shall now examine a few religious images or symbols from various traditions to see if when interpreted or decoded they will support my assumption that death evokes terror and is felt to be hostile to the human enterprise.

(a) Christians

Our first instance is found in the Christian tradition. Following Oscar Cullman, in his book Immortality of the Soul or Resurrection of the Body?, I propose to contrast the death of Jesus as it is contained in the Gospels, and the death of Socrates as it is narrated in Plato's Phaedo. Jesus' death is viewed as a painful and terrifying prospect, not just by the evangelists but -- to the extent that the evangelists are faithfully recording the experience of Jesus -- by Jesus himself. Jesus does not wish to die. Shortly before his capture in the Garden of Gethsemane he prayed, "Father let this cup pass from my hand". 'This cup' means the cup of suffering, the immediate prospect of death with which he is faced. Though he then adds, "Nevertheless thy will be done", Jesus is not serene about his death; he passionately wants to live. We are told that during his prayer, so deep was his agitation, blood poured from his brow like sweat. Certainly this is the portrait of one who feels very acutely the existential anxiety of death.

The picture of Socrates is in sharp contrast. He had been condemned to death on a false charge of corrupting the youth of Athens through his teaching, and the sentence is that he must drink the poison hemlock. His sorrowing friends and family come to see him on the afternoon of his death; the prospect of losing Socrates is acutely painful to them. Though they feel anxiety about death, Socrates appears not to;

he faces his death with equanimity and cheerfulness. At one point he becomes distressed because his wife and her friends are making an irritating noise by their wailing and lamentations, and he asks for the women to be led away. Socrates' brave words reveal his lack of fear in the face of death. He commends the jailor and asks for instructions on the proper way to commit suicide. The jailor complies; Socrates drinks deeply, walks around till his legs become heavy, and lying down, covers himself. At one point he remembers a religious debt, and he asks his friend to discharge it. "Crito, I own a cock to Aesclepius; will you remember to pay the debt?" It might well be claimed that Socrates does not evince anxiety about death.[1] Jesus, by contrast, in his confrontation with death displays a deep distress at the cessation of vital energies, earthly bonds, and appointed tasks.

Admittedly, there are some loose ends in this contrast of the death of Jesus and Socrates. It is, for example, immeasurably less painful to die from poison than from crucifixion. The account we have in the Phaedo does not make execution by poison look like a terribly painful thing. Socrates starts to feel a chill, his limbs grow heavy, and he is compelled to lie down. It does not seem so dreadful an end. But imagine the agony of crucifixion; visualize being bound or spiked to the cross-bar and then raised up to the vertical post to be left there to die. The merciful end to this torture could take several days or up to a week to come.

Moreover, there is a crucial divergence in the death age of the two victims. Jesus is about thirty-three years. At that age most of us would consider the major part of our public and domestic career still lay ahead of us. Socrates, by contrast, had lived seventy years during which time he had experienced the fulfillment of creative enquiry amongst devoted friends and disciples. Clearly, Jesus' death has a poignancy that differentiates it from Socrates'.

Nevertheless, there is a particular power in the portrayal of Jesus' confrontation with his death that conveys the conviction that we are presented here with not just the terror of Jesus' individual circumstances of youth and torture, but with death's universal impact and significance. Certainly, the Christian tradition has interpreted death in this way.

That Jesus' perspective on death became a paradigm or model for Christians is confirmed in a number of places within the scriptures. The following admonition from the letter of James, holds before disciples the constant awareness of their death.

> Come now you who say today or tomorrow we will go into such and such a town and spend a year there and trade and get gain. Whereas you do not know about tomorrow. What is your life? For you are a mist that appears for a little time and then vanishes. Instead you ought to say if the lord wills we shall live and we shall do this or that. As it is you boast in your arrogance. (4:13)

The readers are being reminded that they ought not to put too many eggs into tomorrow's basket. They are constantly to keep in mind the fragility of human existence. This note is sounded again in the well known parable of Jesus:

> And Jesus told the parable saying, The land of a rich man brought forth plentifully, and he thought to himself, what shall I do for I have nowhere to store my crops? And he said I will do this. I will pull down my barns and build larger ones and there I will store all my grain and my goods, and I will say to my soul, soul you have ample goods laid up for many years, take your ease, feast, drink, be merry. God said to him, Fool, this night your soul is required of you. And the things you have prepared whose will they be? (Luke 12:16 ff).

This makes me feel very uneasy because I was recently feeling quite smug about the twelve to thirteen cords of wood that we had chain-sawed and split. I would look out into my backyard and gloatingly survey those enormous stacks of wood, assuring myself that I had enough firewood for three or four winters. For some time I never realized how much I resembled the farmer of Jesus' parable. I could die before I get the chance to burn it -- a very unwelcome prospect but, nevertheless, a salutary reminder of life's evanescence. The parable is a trenchant symbol within the Christian tradition that keeps before its communicants the consciousness that their life can abruptly be taken from them and that decisions should be made in the light of this knowledge. "Fool, this night shall your life be required of you".

Our exploration of the meaning of death contained in some of the stories and images from the Christian tradition continues with a quick scrutiny of a key image for death in I Corinthians 15:26. In the midst of a long passage expositing the teaching about the resurrection of the body, the apostle Paul says that Jesus Christ must reign until he has put all his enemies under his feet. The last enemy is death. This is a clear declaration of the evaluation that the Christian tradition makes upon death, though this is far from the gospel's last word on the subject. If religious traditions appear at times to be rubbing the noses of their devotees in the fact of death it is only because this is a necessary prelude to the therapeutic, transformative answer which they then supply. Accordingly, though Paul urges his readers to recognize the inimical character of death, he does so in the confidence that there is a force greater than the enemy death, and that is the power of the risen Lord. But the evangelical message of hope is predicated on the negative assessment of death as enemy.

Our earlier consideration of the respective ways of Jesus' and Socrates' death leads us to digress momentarily to contrast the anxiety of death with the anxiety of dying. What is more dreaded: the prospect of our annihilation, or the process of actually dying? Both produce anxiety in varying circumstances. Sometimes, perhaps when things seem trialsome and frustrations multiply, the prospect of the end of life might seem welcome, were it not for the pain entailed in leaving it. For such persons the dread of dying itself seems more acute. At other times, it is not the transient period of our dying that induces apprehension, but the contemplation of nothingness. The contemplation of our death discloses the agony of separation from loved persons and the absence of creative work and precious goals. Although, it is fairly easy to distinguish the anxiety of dying from the anxiety of death, it is much more difficult to assess one as being more painful than the other. Nevertheless, I believe that the anxiety of death, that is, apprehension about the apparent end of earthly joys and challenges, the termination of vitality, human

- 13 -

bonds, and ennobling duties, and confrontation with the void, is experienced as most vexatious. Without devaluing or making light of terror about the dying process, the threat that seems to generate most pain and distress is the prospect of nothingness at death.

(b) Buddhists

The same sort of negative estimate of death may be discerned in the Buddhist tradition. Our examination begins with a set of experiences of the Buddha called 'the four sights'. These are frequently represented in the iconography of shrines and monasteries throughout the Buddhist world. The context for the Buddha's four sights (bearing in mind that at that time he was not yet the Buddha, the enlightened one, but Siddartha Gautama, a prince) was a prophecy uttered at the time of his birth. The legends vary somewhat but substantially they agree that the new-born babe would be either a great world emperor, or a great cosmic teacher. His father, resolutely desiring the best for his son and quite intent that his son should become king rather than a preacher, did everything within his power to prevent the destiny of a religious vocation. Siddartha Gautama was sequestered within the grounds of the palace in Lumbini and had no exposure whatsoever to the pain and tragedy of life. Its harsh realities of suffering, decrepitude and death were withheld from him within the pleasurable protective confines of the royal estate.

But one day, so the legend goes, he decided to leave the palace grounds and to walk to the distant city of Kapilavastu. En route with his courtiers, he encountered a strange sight: a person sick with black plague of the groin. Siddartha Gautama was astonished, for he had never until that point in his life seen a sick person. His father had taken care that he did not; no sick person had been allowed within his range of vision in the palace. Siddartha asks:

"What is this, what is this strange sight?"

He is told: "Sickness".

"Sickness, what is that?"

"Sickness is something that sooner or later comes to all human beings."

Siddartha Gautama was astonished that people could live their lives so cavalierly, so oblivious of the prospect of sickness that confronts them throughout life. They continued their walk. A second sight occurred; it was an old man.

"What is this?", the puzzled Siddartha asked.

"This is an aged person."

"Age? What is that?"

"Well that is something to which all human flesh is heir; we grow old, and our vitalities wane."

Again Siddartha Gautama was appalled at the nonchalance of human beings. How incredible it was that in the face of life's palpable suffering they could customarily proceed in such oblivion of it.

They carried on, encountering a funeral cortege bearing a corpse to the burning gat.

Siddartha asks, "What is this?"

"Sire, this is a dead man."

"A dead man, what is that ?"

"We all die; this is a condition which comes to us all, sooner or later."

He felt a dreadful despair that human life which he had theretofore thought of as a joyous enterprise could be so afflicted by sickness, old age, and death.

As they proceeded, they came upon a fourth sight, that of a renunciant or monk (Sanskrit: bhikshu; Pali: bhikku) dedicated to a life of detachment and meditation in order to escape from the suffering of this world and realize the supreme reality beyond space and time. In the vision of the bhikshu, Siddartha glimpsed the way of deliverance from this life of suffering, of illness, senility, and mortality. In the iconography of the Buddhist tradition there is an immediate and constant reminder that life is permeated by death and suffering. The attainment of salvific truth begins with the internalization of this fact of human existence: all must die, and death is one of the ingredients that makes the whole of life sorrowful.

This perspective on death and life conveyed by the four sights may be seen in other aspects of Buddhism. Buddhist monks are enjoined to meditate in graveyards so that in the presence of death they will become disabused of any illusions about life. They will not be deceived by momentary vigours of the body or transient joys because they know the constant horizon of human existence is limitation, culminating in death. It is difficult to get this message across, for a great deal of human energy goes into denying it. Consequently, Buddhists have created a system of discipline and reflection, part of whose function is to break down this normal evasiveness of the human mind. Aspirants, seeking after saving truth, must be obliged to confront the true character of their life which includes the painful element of mortality.

(c) <u>Hindus</u>

In this preliminary hop-skip-and-jump from tradition to tradition isolating symbols that would support our premise that, until counteracted by some coping therapy, the initial human response to death is one of anxiety, we move to the Hindu tradition. Because I intend to deal quite fully with chapter two of the <u>Bhagavad Gita</u> when we come to examine the transformative ripostes to death, I shall refer only briefly now to the <u>Gita's</u> opening scene.

It is the eve of the battle between the Pandavas and the Kauravas, two related families that are vying for supremacy in Bharat or India. Arjuna of the Pandava family and his charioteer Krishna, (who, I think it is fair to disclose, is really the Lord in disguised form), ride out between the serried ranks of the armies. Arjuna surveys his kinsfolk, his cousins, his uncles, on the other side, and contemplates the mighty massacre he knows will ensue. He is so filled with desolation at the prospect of death that he resolves not to be an accomplice to the slaughter. This refusal to take part in the battle entails the repudiation of his warrior's caste duty.

> Ah woe! 'Twas a great wickedness
> That we had resolved to commit,
> In that, through greed for the joys of
>   kingship,
> We undertook to slay our kinsfolk.

Thus saying, Arjuna in the battle
Sat down in the box of the car [the
   chariot],
Letting fall his bow and arrows,
His heart smitten with grief.

This I interpret as a statement, in telescoped form,
that until a transformative message is introduced (as
Krishna will subsequently do) the initial human
reaction to dying and death is one of anxiety and
depression.

From all sides there is a coalescence of judgement
that the human situation is in many ways a painful
predicament, and one of the respects in which it is
most seriously awry is that we all die. That normal,
rational people are deeply vexed by this, both
existential analysis and history of religions testify.

(d) Primitives

I want to complete this sketch of some religious
traditions with a brief allusion to so-called
primitives. There was a time when I wondered if I had
run into a rebuttal of my assumption that death is
initially experienced as pain and problem in G. Van der
Leeuw, Religion in Essence and Manifestation. Van der
Leeuw, in describing the primitives' (or, if one
prefers, preliterate or preindustrial societies')
understanding of death, says that in a sacred context
the dead are felt to be still present; they are not
struck off the roll (213). Death, he says, simply
marks a transition in the mode of being present to the
world of the living. This transition is likened to
that between the stages of life that are separated by
the rite of initiation. In many societies, the passage
from childhood or a profane existence, to adulthood or
a sacred existence, is marked by some ordeal,
constituting a rite de passage. Van der Leeuw claims
that death is nothing more than the kind of transition
that occurs in the rite of passage from adolescence to
adulthood, when the initiates are entitled to hear the
community's sacred stories, learn the myths of the
origins of their people, and hence become warriors or
hunters or whatever their sacred role is.

Two provisos may be entered respecting Van der
Leeuw's interpretation of the primitive's conception of
death. First, it may be that the sacred conception of
the dead as still actively present represents an

alteration of consciousness brought about by a religious tradition whose function it is precisely to transform life from chaos and death to cosmos and redemption. My suspicion is that when Van der Leeuw describes the primitive attitude towards the dead who are still present with the living -- albeit in a different mode -- he is not so much characterizing a primal experience of death, but, rather, death as subsequently interpreted by a tradition whose role it is to deal with the initial anxiety of death.

The same can be said of other traditions. Christian hymns, for example, might well leave the impression that Christians are not at all afraid of death. (As one friend said to me, "Most Christian hymns seem to be saying 'Won't it be wonderful when we're all dead!'") But the view of death evinced there is a transformed view of death; it is not native to consciousness. It is a view of death which the Christian tradition has generated in its devotees by its particular symbol of heavenly consummation. The original existential experience of death, inescapably and universally, is one of anxiety, of dis-ease. Subsequently, traditions may inspire serenity in their devotees with the assurance that there exists a power of being or a sacred reality greater than the destructive power of non-being. When Van der Leeuw describes the primitive's sense that death is not an ominous threat because the dead are not struck off the rolls, he is, I believe, dealing with a consciousness upon which the redemptive religious symbols of primitive culture have already had time to work so as to deliver it from the anxiety of death.

My second reservation is that Van der Leeuw's minimizing of the impact of death by the analogy of initiation rites of passage, implies a misleading understatement of the dramatic transformation effected by initiation. It has been said that a Western adolescent's acquisition of a driver's licence at age sixteen corresponds to a primitive's rite of passage. But an initiation, correctly understood, is not something trivial. To understand the rite of passage, it must be seen in its dramatic, earth-rending quality. It tears apart the pre-existing profane world of the initiate and inserts that person into a new sacred world. It is an awesome and frequently fearful transformation. To assimilate death to the rite of passage and then to fail to see how dramatic and consequential is that rite, leads to an incorrect evaluation of death. I would say that by assimilating death to rites of passage, properly understood, one is not, in fact, minimizing the terror of death but drawing attention to its cruciality. The upshot of these caveats is that Van der Leeuw's assessment of primitive attitudes towards the dead does not invalidate my thesis of death's universal anguish and irrationality.

A scholar who has contributed enormously to our understanding of the meaning of primitive myths, Mircea Eliade, confirms the point I wish to make here. Referring to the terror of time and death, he says in <u>Myths, Dreams, and Mysteries</u> that, "in archaic and 'primitive' culture, <u>this anxiety is not a state in which one can remain</u>; its indispensibility is that of an initiatory experience of a rite of passage .... The issue consists precisely in completing this rite of passage and resolving the crisis by coming out of it at a higher level, awakening to consciousness of a higher mode of being."(243, italics in original). Eliade concedes that even among primitives, death induces anxiety -- a state of affairs so undesirable that one cannot remain there but strives to transcend it through the symbolic agencies made available by one's culture.

Further corroboration of this interpretation of primitive religiousness may be found in the vision of death and life conveyed in the ancient religious tradition of the Mother Goddess that pervaded wide areas of the Mediterranean world throughout a period of possibly 6000 years.

Gunther Zuntz, in his characterization of the Mother Goddess of Sicily in <u>Persephone</u>(1971), indicates structural affinities and antecedents with religious ideas and practices as widely diverse as those in Malta in the third millennium B.C. (contemporaneous with the civilization of Sumer and the Old Kingdom in Egypt) and Catal Huyuk in Asia Minor, C. 6000 B.C.

He begins with the carvings on two stone slabs, originating in the 2nd or 3rd millennium B.C., which guarded the entrances of graves at Castellucio, Sicily. The carvings consist of two pairs of spirals. The first or top pair is a symbolic representation of the Mother, the spirals suggesting her breasts. The lower spirals connected with an angular bar represent the male's testes and the phallus penetrating the Goddess.

The meaning is that even in the presence of death -- at the grave itself -- the creative, life-giving power of the divine Mother is still salvifically active to transcend death and bestow new life. As Zuntz exclaims, "The act of begetting depicted on the door of the grave."

A similar worldview centred on the cultus of the Mother (probably chronologically prior) is manifested in the temples of Malta. Their trefoil form, comprising two elongated curved structures in kidney bean shape, surmounted by a smaller apse, convey the image of the Mother. The apse represents the head, the next distended and curved shape is her breasts, and the lower one is her hips and womb. "These buildings reproduce, in a fixed symbolic form, the body of the Great Mother", says Zuntz (8).

The cosmological and existential meaning of the artifacts of the Mother cultus is conveyed by the decorative images that embellish the shrines excavated at Catal Huyuk on the Konya plain. Frescoes depicting vultures, images of death, hover over headless (that is, dead) human bodies. Thus is the existential threat of death kept before the gaze of the devotees.

The antidote to death is also mediated by this primitive iconography in the form of the Mother in the act of giving birth to a bull. "Her progeny is the bull, the essential begetter ... asserting his power to overcome death" (14). Further, "The begetter and the parturient: these two are constantly undoing the work of the vultures -- whose prey is the perishable flesh ... (14).

The opposition between life and death, between eros and thanatos, is clear. The vultures oppose the Mother and her taurine offspring. Death in this cultus and perspective is described by Zuntz as 'perennial antagonist' (15). The tradition, however, provides not only insight into the reality and meaning of death, but also its resolution. The Mother -- intrinsically life herself, and life-giving -- conquers death. "The sum of this religious experience was comprised in devotion to the Goddess. Ever parturient, she is the perennial source of life" (15). Again, "The whole of the power that originates and preserves life tends to be found in the Female deity" (15). She is "The superior antagonist of death and mother of all life" (p.17). Death and life are in polar opposition -- death is, or would be, existential terror -- were it not for the superiority of the Mother's life-bestowing power.

Though widely separated in time and space these cults of the Mother, "realize the divinity of life eternal in the form of the 'Mother of all'; they acknowledge the ineluctable lot of death awaiting every one of the Mother's creatures; they sense and lament its irretrievable horror yet are passionately certain of the Mother's -- of Life's superiority and permanence" (21). The religious experience of primal peoples corroborates the judgement that profound apprehension in the face of death is basic to human existence -- requiring an efficacious power to counter death.

The episode which I now narrate to conclude this section, contributed to the formulation of this study's thesis of the universality of the human characterization of death as dreadful enemy. Notwithstanding outsiders' facile stereotypes of religious fatalism, heaven, nirvana, rebirth, eternal soul, etc., the fact remains that death -- especially of our children -- is rarely faced without a greater or lesser degree of profound anxiety and despair.

In 1973, trekking from Katmandu to Mount Everest, we arrived at the hamlet of Nuntale (7200 feet) comprised of two stone huts just as dusk settled on the mountains. The Sherpas who inhabit the highlands of eastern Nepal are devotees of Tibetan Buddhism. Inside the darkened interior of the larger hut, three wine-robed lamas were busy in the performance of a ritual. Two peered at the leaves of a worn hymn book from which they chanted, while another played cymbals and rang a bell intermittently. One of them occasionally thumped a drum hanging from the ceiling. This ceremony which was in progress when we arrived, continued for another fifteen minutes. From time to time a youth, grasping a wicker shield and <u>kukri</u> (large angled knife) and crouching beside the seated lamas, would suddenly leap up brandishing his weapons and whack his knife against the shield and the doorposts -- all the while shouting defiant threats into the gathering gloom outside. Several times a woman approached a boat-like model on the floor about two feet in length holding a dozen small figurines with diamond shaped flags. She threw a corn offering on it on one occasion; on another she placed children's clothing over it. When the hymn book's last leaf was turned, the youth with the kukri led the way charging out of the house and up the mountain side from where we had just come. Right on his heels was a young man (whom we subsequently learned was the father of two small sick children) bearing the model, followed by one of the lamas clanging his cymbals.

We were ready to leave about 6.15 the next morning when one of the trekkers who had slept in the dwelling next door to us urgently called me to witness the practices of the witch doctor (as he called him) which were going on in his hut. The mother in this drama of demon excorcism sat on the bed holding one very sick baby of about six to her breast while another of about four or five lay almost comatose on the bed under some dirty blankets. The exorciser sat on the floor a few feet away. (They asked us if we had medicine for the children but we explained our medicines were mainly for the stomach and not for coughs in the chest. At various times along the trail we had dispensed some medicines -- mainly Lomotil for diarrhea and ointment for small wounds).

Planted into a crack in the floor boards was a two foot branch from which hung several prayer streamers. On the floor before the exorcist were two brass bowls into which flowers, rice, and glowing coals were periodically placed and sprinkled with water. Alternatively, water, petals and rice were sprinkled on the mother and two children. The father -- whose charge up the mountain we had witnessed the previous evening -- hovered nearby being helpful by handing coals with a tongs to the practitioner who all the while kept up incantations in a manner of sincere concern. He was youngish, about thirty, dressed in ordinary clothes, quite ragged and dirty. Abruptly the exorciser seized the bowls and ran out and up the slope followed by the father. The aim clearly seemed to be to banish the disease from the young victims to the wilderness beyond.

The distress of the parents at this assault of sickness and death upon their young children was palpable. The magical, therapeutic resources of their religious culture were being called upon to forestall the evil enemy death.

3. Description and Truth Claims

Our approach is, for the most part, a combination of philosophy and history of religions. It is philosophical in that it engages in reflection on the meaning of human existence to ascertain if systematic patterns can be discerned. If one wishes, what I term 'philosophy' in this context might be alternatively designated as phenomenology or soft social science. It is historical in that the deposit that has been left to us in sacred scripture, doctrinal teaching, image, myth and ritual by various religious traditions of mankind, is seriously examined to uncover the cosmological insights contained therein.

Exception might be taken to my approach precisely on the ground that it is not sufficiently scientific. I am not entirely clear what criteria would have to be met to warrant designating an undertaking in human enquiry as 'scientific'. There are harder and softer degrees of science depending on whether the investigator works with test tubes in a laboratory, or with human beings in an interview schedule. I am disinclined to introduce the notion of science in my treatment of death and afterlife. Ernest Becker, the author of The Denial of Death, sought, as his life's aim, a synthesis of theology and science. He came at science as an anthropologist or as a social psychologist. In an interview with Sam Keen shortly before his death, at the age of 49, published in Psychology Today, he reiterated his intention to achieve a confluence of the insights of theology and those of psychology. Clearly, some are not embarrassed to use the term science respecting their investigation of death. I do not myself claim scientific method for this enquiry because science for many people suggests an intellectual activity that has very strong demonstrative and predictive powers. A scientific claim derives its authority from the fact that the conditions or results it describes are, in principle, replicable anywhere and at any time. As far as I can determine we do not have that competency in the kind of intellectual exploration about death and afterlife in which we are engaged.

Still I want to insist that the premise upon which I am basing our exploration -- namely that death is an existential threat to which the symbol systems of religion seek to give, by varying strategies, a therapeutic or transformative answer -- is not a capricious or ungrounded premise. There is, I have argued, strong confirmation of my premise from the perspective of philosophical anthropology (Ernest Becker might have thought it was soft scientific anthropology) or existentialist analysis. Such analysis discloses that for most people the prospect of death is not viewed as a natural event, if by 'natural' is meant an entirely acceptable event in the context of the universe unfolding as it should.

Moreover, this interpretation of death is the result not only of the reflections of pivotal thinkers like Paul Tillich, the philosophical theologian, and Clifford Geertz, the anthropologist, but also, as far as I am able to discern, the discovery of the great religious traditions of the world. While historical consensus is not incontrovertible evidence for the truth of any particular claim, it does provide a prima facie confirmation -- especially when the matters entailed are fundamental human problems and projects.

But ultimately the existentialist dilemma cannot be escaped; ascertaining the validity of these alternative solutions to the question of the meaning of human life requires that risky decisions be made. Lacking demonstrative power; lacking, for example, the ability to prove that the immortal soul is the true doctrine, and the resurrection of the body a fanciful one; or again, lacking the ability to demonstrate whether a personal God counts the hairs on our heads, or our lives are ruled by mechanistic forces which are fundamentally detached from human concerns and yearnings, we are forced back upon life stances whose logical force is, at best, probability. Being unable to prove the matter one way or the other, people ultimately have to decide that (A) is true and (B) false. Or, if they can work out a synthetic alchemy, they may decide both (A) and (B) are true; or, possibly, that both (A) and (B) are false. But, in any case, they cannot frame their answer in such a way that it constitutes an irrefutable proof to someone who comes to it as a stranger. There seems no way of getting around this existentialist dilemma that when dealing with this kind of human truth a practical, unproven and unprovable decision must be made. This is not blind, not totally arbitrary; it is generally made on the basis of certain clues. But such clues do not constitute knock-down evidence; rather, they are provocative and evocative. The obligation remains to make a subjective decision for truth which in the old

days used to be called faith. Our main task, however,
is not the settling of the truth question; its burden
is the description of alternative human understandings
of death and afterlife -- 'afterlife' being used in
this context as a general term for a religious means of
dealing transformatively with death's threat.

NOTES

1. I deliberately put the issue of Socrates' feelings towards his death in a problematic way ("it might well be claimed that Socrates does not evince anxiety about death.") Clearly, it would help my thesis if Socrates shared Jesus's anxiety about his end. I was delighted to read Paul Ramsey's ironic comment on what he called Plato's "idealized account of the death of Socrates":

> It should be remembered that we know not whether Socrates' hands trembled as he yet bravely drank the hemlock, no more than we know how Isaac experienced dying when "fullness of years" came upon him. Secondary accounts of these matters are fairly untrustworthy.

REFERENCES

Cullmann, Oscar
1958 Immortality of the Soul or Resurrection of the Dead? The Witness of the New Testament. London: Epworth Press.

Eliade, Mircea
1967 Myths, Dreams, and Mysteries: The Encounter Between Contemporary Faiths and Archaic Realities. New York: Harper & Row. First published in French, 1957.

Geertz, Clifford
1965 "Religion as a Cultural System". In Michael Banton, ed., Anthropological Approaches to the Study of Religion. London: Tavistock Publications.

Leach, Edmund R.
1966 "Ritualization in Man in Relation to Conceptual and Social Development." Philosophical Transactions of the Royal Society of London. Reprinted in William A. Lessa and Evon Z. Vogt, Reader in Comparative Religion: An Anthropological

     Approach. New York: Harper & Row, revised
     ed. 1972.

Tillich, Paul
  1952 The Courage to Be. New Haven: Yale
     University Press.

Van der Leeuw, Gerardus
  1963 Religion in Essence and Manifestation. New
     York: Harper & Row. The German original
     Phanomenologie der Religion published in
     1933.

Zuntz, Gunther
  1971 Persephone: Three Essays on Religion and
     Thought in Magna Graecia. London: Oxford
     University Press.

Temple of the cult of the Mother-Goddess in Malta. The architecture symbolizes the fecund body of the Great Mother.

Stone-slab carving from graves of Castelluccio, Sicily representing the generative power of the Mother-Goddess.

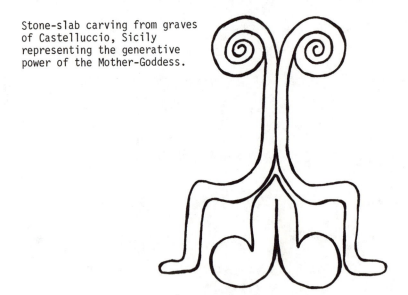

CHAPTER TWO

CONSTITUENTS OF THE DREAD AND DENIAL OF DEATH

1. Why is Death Dreaded?

We have noted how the history of religions and existential analysis converge to corroborate the premise that death is experienced as a dilemma, as a source of bafflement, as pain and paradox. The question is now raised as to why this convergence should exist. Why should there be such near unanimity in this negative way of perceiving death? We turn to a consideration of some of the constituents of dread.

(a) The Loss of Love and Earthly Joy

Some of the answers are transparent. Death means, or appears to mean, the rupture of the bonds of love. Most human value systems affirm love as the greatest gift, and the tragedy is that it apparently ends with bodily dissolution. We seem to know intuitively -- until some message of deliverance assures us to the contrary -- that our bodily existence is essential to our relationship with other persons. Our bodily organs enable communication. Verbal communication, for example, entails sound waves emitted from the larynx falling upon and vibrating the ear drums and then, by some complex neural electricity, being transmitted to the brain and registering as meaning. But communication is the collusion not only of sounds but also of bodily gestures, grimaces and contortions. So obvious is the role of physical sexuality in the language of love that it needs only to be mentioned to clinch the argument that bodily life is intrinsic to love.

Bodily impressions are of highest importance even in the earliest year of an infant's development. The way even the most recently born infant is held, very quickly communicates to that infant whether the cosmos is a secure or a threatening place and, consequently, whether the appropriate stance on the world should be one of pervasive trust or suspicion.

James Carse presents a cogent statement of the way in which death as social separation implicates us in personal meaninglessness as well. His argument runs as follows:

1. To be a person is to live in a dialectical relation of autonomy and dependence with others. "To be a person we must exist in ... a web of connectedness with other persons."

2. Death is not only organic destruction but, most significantly, the loss of the other in relation with whom we have received our own personhood. "Death, therefore, is primarily to be understood as the irreversible damage to the web of connectedness between persons ... What we experience is not death of another as death, but the sudden tearing of the fragile web of existence." (Carse 1980: 4, italics in original).

3. Death, accordingly, is simultaneously a cause of grief at the termination of social and historical continuity, and an attack on the meaningfulness of our subjective selfhood which is correlated with that social web.

Paul Tillich, in The Courage To Be, says that we instinctively sense that there is a correlation between the self and the world and that when one member disappears the other member also disappears. In other words, death entails the disappearance of the body; with the body gone the human being also appears to have vanished and that, in turn, implies the annihilation of the world. Do we wonder why death generates such profound anxiety? Death seems to mean not only the loss of self, but the loss of all.

At six years of age our son asked me about a moderately elderly man on our street, "Will Mr. Gilbert die?". I gave some characteristically profound adult answer which did not, however, assuage his inchoate anxiety. He then asked, "Where will he go?" Already our young son had caught on that human survival has got something to do with bodies, and that if the body is not visible when death has occurred, then there had better be a body someplace else. For if there is not, then Mr. Gilbert probably no longer exists and relationship is impossible. So I gave some answer --

which still left our son unhappy. A third question
soon followed: "Will God bring him back to this
world?" A six year old evinces a sneaking suspicion
that human existence is correlated with bodily
existence. In effect, the youngster is saying,
"I understand what living means in this world. But I
am not sure that a strange existence somewhere else
under different conditions would be truly living."
Still a fourth question ensued: "Where are the mean
men when they die?" I had earlier said something that
suggested conditional resurrection of the righteous
only. Accordingly, he wanted to know also the destiny
of the wicked!

These questions reveal the resistance of young
minds, unconfused by the evasive subtleties of
theology, to being fobbed-off with vague answers about
life and death. Life for them means earthly, bodily
life. Since death means the apparent dissolution of
the body, then hope for a heavenly afterlife (or,
conversely, the threat of post-mortem punishment)
requires the restoration of the deceased to the sort of
bodily life we are familiar with on earth. The
alternative is nothingness.

Death obviously signals the termination of
creative tasks -- for those who want to write the great
book, paint a masterpiece, discover a cancer cure or
lead a movement for national liberation, and also those
who simply want to build a log cabin or learn how to
ski. Death seems to write _finis_ to all these
aspirations for creative undertaking. The steady
horizon of death means one may not get the chance.

Finally, death means the annihilation of vitality
and bodily joys. The body is a source of much
vexation admittedly, but also, paradoxically, the
source of much joy from walking among snow-capped
mountains, swimming in a limpid lake, or sharing a good
meal with friends. The annihilation of the body
announces the end of these joys.

(b) The Dread of Weakness and Nothingness

Death may be dreaded and denied on different
levels and for different reasons. It may generate
anxiety, Becker suggests, because of an inherent and
universal biological disposition to resist destruction.
In its instinctive impulse to live, the biological
organism resists death. We are genetically programmed

to drive for biological self-preservation. The natural dynamic of the living organism is to maintain itself, to expand, to grow. Death is the negation of this instinctive drive, and its acknowledgment is, therefore, resisted even at the biological level.

The primordial dread of death arises also, according to Becker, from humanity's dual nature. We live an existential paradox between animal and spirit or symbolic self. The animal element of our make-up contradicts the transcendence and sovereignty of our symbolic self. This contradiction is exemplified by our present enquiry into death! We transcend our limitations and explore the mystery of life and death, on the one hand, and yet, on the other, we are mocked by indigestion, allergies, or migraine headache, to mention only our most mild ailments. Because death is the chief symbol of our limitation, our dependency, our vulnerability and extinction, it is both feared and repressed. This insight that death is feared and consequently denied, not only because of its intrinsic painful liabilities but also because of its symbolic power to remind us of our human weakness and futility, is shared by Aries. He says, "Decomposition is the sign of man's failure" (Aries 1974:42)[1].

2. The Denial of Death

Human life, I have argued, is marked by existential anxiety, a universal and ultimately inescapable uneasiness about our finitude, epitomized by our mortality. And yet, paradoxically, death is widely denied.

(a) Why is Death Denied?

I say the denial of death is paradoxical. This is certainly true when it is viewed against the background of its capacity to generate universal anxiety. How can something that is universal be evaded? And yet it is; and this fact explains my characterization of death denial as paradoxical.

There is, however, another perspective from which the denial of death is not a paradox but an inevitable, logical consequence. If the delineation of the impact of death upon human values, desires and hopes given above is on target, then it is scarcely mysterious that humans should want to deny death. If death means the loss of loving relation and the abyss of annihilation, it should be expected that all but the most heroic should want to look the other way to avoid confronting the terror.

The repression of death, Becker argues, is borne out by psycho-analytic investigation. If Becker is right in his analysis of Freud's doctrine of sexual repression as, in reality, repression of the consciousness of death, then it is evident that the denial of death is not a peculiarly modern phenomenon, but has always, to a greater or lesser extent, characterized humans. On this interpretation, death-repression becomes an intrinsic dynamic of human consciousness analogous to the way in which Freudians regarded sexual repression to be. In this same vein, Leo Tolstoy's literary presentation of Ivan Ilych's denial of the imminence of his death also supports the view that the evasion of the pain and perplexity of death is a universal psychological quality. Becker analyzes sexual phenomena like anality, oedipus complex, castration complex, and penis envy, and concludes that the explicity sexual explanation of these modes of behaviour is a disguise for our true existential apprehension of limitation culminating in our death.

Though death induces existential or universal anxiety, it should be noted that the denial of the unpalatable fact of our death is not historically constant. In contemporary life, this denial has become overwhelmingly the case. In addition to the universal biological, social, and psychological motives for dreading and denying death, there is in our own time -- to which the term 'modernity' is usually applied -- a further cultural reinforcement of this evasiveness.

In striking language, Aries draws attention to the rapid, contemporary domination of the attitude of denial towards death, though his characterization of it as "an absolutely unheard-of phenomenon" runs counter to the existential outlook espoused in this present treatment of death.

> In our day, in approximately a third of a century, we have witnessed a brutal revolution in traditional ideas and feelings, a revolution so brutal that social observers have not failed to be struck by it. It is really an absolutely

unheard-of phenomenon. Death, so omnipresent in the past that it was familiar, would be effaced, would disappear. It would become shameful and forbidden (Aries 1974:85).

The reason for this evasion is that modern culture itself has taken on the characteristics of religion -- albeit a secular one -- whose dominant perceptions and values are hostile to the candid acknowledgement of human mortality. The dominant religious system of modern culture -- secular humanism -- is threatened by the reality of death in a way that earlier religious traditions were not. The universal, existential anxiety of death coalesces in the modern world with this system whose basic perspective is challenged if not invalidated by the reality of human finitude, quintessentially seen in death.

The chief article of faith of this modern, secular tradition -- which is the operative religion of our time -- is human mastery. Bacon's epigram "Knowledge is Power" is its cardinal confession. Through technology, which scientific knowledge makes possible, the human race is guaranteed control of its destiny.[2] One can readily perceive why the reality of death is unpalatable to the religion of modernity. It calls into question and even mocks the fundamental tenet of modernity, namely, the autonomy, mastery and progress of humankind. Death imposes the realization of our human weakness and limitation. There is, after all, at least one major area that remains outside human control -- this is our ultimate span of days. All our struggles and achievements are in prospect of being ridiculed by the inevitability of our extinction.

So threatening is death's attack on the faith of modernity that super-heroic efforts are called forth to deal with it. Technology, which has bequeathed so many apparent benefits in medicine, transportation, agriculture, industry and communication, is called upon for its ultimate legacy -- the abolition of death. And so we had the emergence of the technique of cryogenics (fortunately not so much heard of recently) in which the deceased body is put in deep freeze to be thawed and restored to life when medical technology reaches the point of being able to treat the disease or injury from which the subject had died. But even the modest phenomenon of power blackouts during sleet storms and strikes, should serve to expose the inadequacies of this technical innovation to pluck the barb from death: What happens when the power fails?[3]

This discussion of the role of culture in shaping attitudes towards death provides the occasion for resuming the debate on the first of the two central theses of this present enquiry. It might be thought that my assertion of a universal, inherent attitude towards death is contradicted by historical investigations such as that of Philippe Aries in Western Attitudes Towards Death: From The Middle Ages to the Present and Ivan Illich in Limits to Medicine. Aries' intent is precisely to show the historical changes in perspectives on death, ranging from the early Middle Ages' sense of familiarity and relative ease in the face of death ("tamed death") to the interdiction of death ("forbidden death") manifest in modern, technological culture.[4]

It should, however, by now be clear that it is no part of my enterprise to deny the role of culture in modifying the primordial, existential experience of death as threat. If fact, it is my thesis that the intention of religious cultures or symbol systems is precisely the ultimate alteration of this primordial death terror in order to achieve some sort of transformed beatitude for its participants. Moreover, it is part of my argument above that the culture of modernity exacerbates (as, of course, Aries also argues) the denial of death. Nevertheless, I contend that reflective analysis and religious testimony combine in support of the view that beneath all culturally modified meanings of death, there is an antecedent, existential awareness of death as source of human pain and bafflement, and a corresponding endemic denial of death.

Although in this brief book, Aries does not specify the meaning of his belief in "the great forces of inertia which reduce the real impact of innovations" (Aries 1974:2), it may well be that what he has in mind are those human psychic dispositions which are more or less permanent in the species and which I typically designate as existential conditions.[5]

Aries goes on to indicate the cultural reinforcement of the psychic disposition towards denial in a way resembling my analysis set out above. But whereas I emphasize the motif of confident mastery in modern, technological culture which is threatened by a forthright encounter with death, Aries draws attention to the 'euphoric' dimension of modernity, especially in its American form. The motivation for the 'lie' about death was "a new sentiment characteristic of modernity: one must avoid...the disturbance and the overly strong and unbearable emotion caused by the ugliness of dying and by the very presence of death in the midst of a happy life, for it is henceforth given that life is always happy or should always seem to be so." (Aries 1974:87).

The function of religions historically has been to overcome this endemic evasion of our mortality and finitude by presenting to the imagination stories and images whose point is to remind their devotees that they will die. The religious traditions prevailing in earlier periods were rarely captivated by visions of Promethean human capacities, and accordingly, were less reluctant to stare death in the face.

Granted, having forced their followers to confront their mortality, the religious traditions then proceeded, in one way or another, to deliver a therapeutic message in which the anxiety of death is vanquished. The Christian tradition, for example, though pessimistic in its assessment of empirical human nature with its mortal flaw, has a trump card to play against the enemy of death, in its conviction about God's eschatological triumph over sin and death in the second coming of Christ. Accordingly, the denial of death, so evident in today's dominant culture of modernity was far less pervasive in times when the Christian ethos predominated.

(b) How Is Death Denied?

Our purpose now is to examine some of the particular processes by which human beings have effected this denial. One way of denial is by naturalizing death. By this I mean that death is seen as something that can be assimilated to the natural rhythms of sunrise and sunset; of spring and fall. There are rhythms in nature where growth gives way to maturation, and maturation to decay, and from the seeds of this decay come new life. Human beings share these natural rhythms. Accordingly, rather than viewing death as a source of terror and perplexity, it is seen as an unfrightening natural phase, occurring as it should because life can unfold in no other way.

Another way of naturalizing death is to see death as a necessary ingredient of the evolutionary process. There would be no passage from lower to higher species if there were no death because the original inhabitants would preempt the environment. The phenomenon of death allows the disappearance of certain species and the emergence of other, more adaptable, higher species. Death (so the argument runs) rather than being a source of terror ought to be respected, even welcomed, as one of the instrumentalities by which nature works out its evolutionary purpose.

Death is further denied by <u>romanticizing</u> it. This again takes various forms. Many years ago in a church bulletin I found a little poem which seemed to me excessively romantic, even at that early stage of understanding. I was uncomfortable with what I thought was the superficial devaluation of the meaning of death by a facile assuagement of bereavement.

"Death is only an old door in a garden wall.
On quiet hinges, it gives at dusk, when the thrushes call.
Along the lintel are green leaves.
Beyond the light lies still;
Many weary and willing feet go over that sill;
There's nothing to trouble any heart,
Nothing to fear at all;
Death is only an old door in a garden wall.

Admittedly there may be a certain legitimacy to this sentiment, and I have to confess that perhaps I am now abusing it for pedagogical purposes. One could say that sort of thing, but not as an initial reaction to the reality of death. Perhaps after the internalization of a religious transformative message, devotees might come to the point where they would want to say, "Death is only an old door in a garden wall" and "There is nothing to trouble any heart -- nothing to fear at all". But if I have been right in expositing the premise that death induces existential anxiety, then the verse is simply false. It is really a form of repression as Ernest Becker would say; it is a way of dealing with death by romanticizing its anxiety out of existence.[6]

Nietzsche, the German philosopher who died in 1900, says things that sometimes strike me as romanticizing death. He articulates a vision of the superman in which human beings are summoned to transcend themselves, to express their will to power, to give vent to their desire to grow, to create, to expand into the universe. And this expression should take place even at the cost of life. He argues that for the superman, the person who has learned to transcend the mediocrity, deception, limitation, and conventionality of the herd and the morality of the resentful, death holds no fear. The worst destiny for the superman is the confinement of wooden bourgeois life, and he is, accordingly, prepared to sacrifice even survival for the sake of the will to power. Though I find Nietzsche a highly provocative thinker, I draw back from this romanticizing of death. The insight that death is inexplicable terror is more compelling.

Another way that people deny death, if they do not naturalize it, and if they do not romanticize it, is by ignoring it. It was Pascal, the French, Christian existentialist who said that since human beings could do nothing about death they chose to ignore it. This is done in various ways. It is done, for example, in contemporary, North American funeral practices. I hasten to add, that this is not a professional attack on morticians but on the culture that requests and supports their practices. I do not think the mortician inspires society's interpretation of death and its ways of dealing with it. He is basically in the business of serving a social demand that arises from society's discomfort with death to the point of repression. The funeral practices that encourage us to evade the reality of someone having succumbed to death, are grounded in a pervasive cultural evasion of death that reflects a fundamental value of modernity, namely, the Promethean spirit of mastery through technology.

In my days as a parish minister, I officiated at funerals where the conspiracy to evade death was overwhelming. I remember caskets set in blue painted alcoves perforated so that the lights of stars would shine through the ersatz sky. Fronds and palms, their green symbolizing eternal life, were scattered around. To top it all, living waters, real miniature streams, flowed down the back wall of the apse in which the casket was set. What was the point here? Some good things could be said about it: it was attempting to use almost universal symbols like green plants and running water to convey to the mourners a message of eternal life. Some less savoury interpretations, however, can be put on it; it can be perceived as a lamentable attempt to evade the reality of death. This is confirmed when one notes how the cosmetician's art is brought to consummate perfection in order to disguise the fact that death has taken place. The cosmetician's skill masks from viewers the fragility of the accident victim's flesh and blood, and conspires to make the corpse look not so bad after all. These practices reflect our culture's prevailing embarrassment, confusion and apprehension at death, and its desire to evade it by repressing its reality.

William May, in Perspectives on Death (1969) points out that not only funeral practices but also other social institutions reflect our society's attitude towards death, including our institutions of healing. Very few persons have actually seen someone die. May charges that our institutions collaborate in this societal denial of death. The terminally ill are not only hidden away in large hospitals, but are concealed in special wards. A friend refers -- not out of any insensitivity, but using the common language of the hospital at which she works -- to a certain ward as the 'vegetable patch', where people, whose brains are so damaged recovery is not expected, are sequestered. Elizabeth Kubler-Ross has pointed out the reason for this medical avoidance of dying patients. Sickness and death signify the failure of the medical profession to do that which justifies its existence, namely, the healing of sickness and injury. Terminal disease and accidental death are stark reminders of limits on human capacities to heal persons. Only masochists want to be reminded of their failures, or, alternatively, very saintly persons who know that humility may lead to wisdom. Our society's medical institutions where most ordinary citizens are excluded from the process of dying, serve to reinforce the denial of death.

The same judgement may be made respecting our homes for the aged. What used to happen in a family milieu, once upon a time, now happens in special institutions where the aged and debilitated are isolated so they will not be routinely visible to threaten our comfort. Just as Siddartha Gautama's father insulated him against the pain of human existence, even so the sick and dying are not allowed to challenge our optimism or to prick the bubble of repression that prevents us from grappling with the reality of death and the deep anxiety which it engenders.

NOTES

1. These sentiments are encapsulated in this
    citation:

    The dread of death is the dread of
    oblivion, of there being only empty room
    in one's stead. Kubler-Ross writes that
    for the dying, death means the loss of
    every loved one, total loss of
    everything that constituted the self
    in its world, separation from every
    experience, even from future possible,
    replacing experiences -- nothingness
    beyond. (Ramsey 1975: 84).

2. A sub-tradition of the religion of modernity is to
    be seen in modern health services. Cf., "Through
    the medicalization of death, health care has
    become a monolithic world religion whose tenets
    are taught in compulsory schools and whose ethical
    rules are applied to a bureaucratic restructuring
    of the environment...." (Illich 1977:208-9).

3. Alan Harrington makes a case for the technological
    conquest of death in <u>The Immortalist</u> (1969). He
    argues that tedium may be eliminated and
    enthusiasm for life maintained "by a system of
    designed sleeps and programmed reincarnations.
    Techniques of freezing or administered hibernation
    will permit us to rest for designated periods
    between an endless variety of lives and careers."
    Cited in Carse (1980:3).

4. Illich pursues a similar theme in his chapter
    entitled "Death Against Death". He writes: "We
    have seen death turn from God's call into a
    'natural' event and later into a 'force of
    nature'; in a further mutation it had turned into
    an 'untimely' event when it came to those who were
    not both healthy and old. Now it had become the
    outcome of specific diseases certified by the
    doctor." (<u>Limits to Medicine</u> 1977:199).

5. This is not to deny that some problems remain in
    attempting to reconcile Aries, views with my own.
    What sense are we to make of his claim that the
    eighteenth century, evidenced in the Marquis de
    Sade, produces a mutation in death attitudes that
    is unparalleled. "This idea of rupture is

something completely new ... From now on it would be thought of as a <u>break</u>." (Aries 1974: 57-8; italics in original). In my perception, the experience of death as rupture or break is not a culturally and historically unique emergent, but, rather, an experience inherent in human consciousness until such times as it is replaced or modified by a therapeutic religious or other cultural message.

6.   cf., "Death for an older person should be a beautiful event. There is beauty in birth, growth, fullness of life and then, equally so, in the tapering off and final end. There are analogies all about us. What is more beautiful than the spring budding of small leaves; then the fully-leaved tree in summer; and then in the beautiful brightly colored autumn leaves gliding gracefully to the ground? So it is with humans." (Draft document on euthanasia by the Council for Christian Social Action of the United Church of Christ, 1972. Cited in Ramsey 1975: 85.).

REFERENCES

Aries, Philippe.
    1974 <u>Western Attitudes Toward Death: From The Middle Ages to the Present.</u> Baltimore: The Johns Hopkins University Press.

Becker, Ernest.
    1973 <u>The Denial of Death.</u> New York: The Free Press.

Carse, James P.
    1980 <u>Death and Existence: A Conceptual History of Human Mortality.</u> New York: John Wiley & Sons.

Harrington, Alan
    1969 <u>The Immortalist.</u> New York.

Illich, Ivan
    1977 <u>Limits of Medicine, Medical Nemesis: The Expropriation of Health.</u> Harmondsworth, England: Penquin Books.

May, William
    1969 "The Sacral Power of Death in Contemporary

Society" in Liston O Mills, ed., *Perspectives on Death.* Nashville: Abingdon Press.

Ramsey, Paul
    1975 "The Indignity of 'Death with Dignity' in Peter Steinfels and Robert Veatch, eds., *Death Inside Out: The Hastings Centre Report.* New York: Harper & Row.

CHAPTER THREE

THE DEATH OF IVAN ILYCH

Our concern now is with an analysis of the anxiety of dying and death as these are presented in Tolstoy's story "The Death of Ivan Ilych." One hesitates at the beginning of an exploration of death and afterlife to exposit at length "The Death of Ivan Ilych" for to do so is to risk saying all that needs to be said. Nearly all the important themes of our analysis of the meaning of death and the possibility of a hopeful answer to it are adumbrated in this story. The clarity and comprehensiveness with which the artist lays bare to our imagination and our understanding the anxieties of death, meaninglessness and guilt, and further, his acute analyses of the psychology of sickness and the dynamics of the dying process, are truly awesome.

The stages through which Kubler-Ross has discovered many dying people pass, are here depicted with acute fidelity, but perhaps more skillfully than has she, in that these experiences of denial, anger, bargaining, despair and acceptance are more realistically shown -- not as successive stages more or less neatly transcended in order -- but as fluctuating, repeated states of consciousness. At least this is the case until Ivan Ilych reaches his final acceptance of death.

The question regarding the relative weight to be given to the anxiety of dying over against the anxiety of death is dealt with perceptively. Both of these anxieties are vividly exposed within a single paragraph.

"Left alone Ivan Ilych groaned not so much with pain, terrible though that was, as from mental anguish. Always and forever the same, always these endless days and nights. If only it would come quicker! If only what would come quicker? Death, darkness? ... No, No! Anything rather than death!"(161).

Note the contrast. First, there is the lament about the intensity of pain -- the agony and anxiety of the dying process. But this is immediately contrasted with the abyss, the nothingness of death. In the face of what it might mean to be finally and irrevocably extinguished, Ivan Ilych chooses the pain and anguish of dying over the terror and enigma of death. This choice is indicated in a number of other places:

> It's not a question of appendix or kidney, but of life and ... death. Yes, life was there and now it is going, going and I cannot stop it. Yes. Why deceive myself? Isn't it obvious to everyone but me that I'm dying, and that it's only a question of weeks, days ... it may happen this moment. There was light and now there is darkness, I was here and now I'm going there! Where?"
>
> A chill came over him, his breathing ceased, and he felt only the throbbing of his heart.
>
> "When I am not, what will there be? There will be nothing. Then where shall I be when I am no more? Can this be dying? No, I don't want to."
>
> He jumped up and tried to light the candle, felt for it with trembling hands, dropped candle and candlestick on the floor, and fell back on his pillow. (152-3)

There you see clearly the apprehension that is induced by the prospect of nothingness. It is, as I suggested earlier, an apprehension that is reinforced by a realistic anxiety about the cessation of creativity, the sundering of social bonds, even fragmentary as they may be for Ivan Ilych. There is also the anxiety generated by the sense of one's work being halted prematurely. But in the case of Ivan Ilych, who has not found much fulfillment in the relationship of love, who has come to find his work tedious, and who, in his preoccupation with bourgeois pursuits, has not experienced much creativity in life, the apprehension of death is induced mainly by the prospect of the abyss -- of annihilation and nothingness.

Something else which should be noted is the interconnection of the anxiety of death with the anxieties of meaninglessness and guilt. Earlier we discussed Paul Tillich's analysis of the human condition or, as it is sometimes called the existential situation. According to this analysis which was echoed by Geertz and receives confirmation in the history of religions, life is characterized by anxiety about fate and death, that is, the threat of subjection and limitation by powers over which we have no control; the anxiety of meaninglessness, that is, the prospect that there is neither coherence nor value in the universe and, finally, the experience of guilt, the sense that our life has been given as a gift which we have trivialized and wasted. It would be a mistake to suppose that these are quite separate experiences, and in the death of Ivan Ilych we see how interrelated they are in fact. The dread of death is exacerbated by the prospect of meaninglessness. Why should death have to exist at all? Why should I die? These questions emerge once the stage of denial has been passed, once one has gone beyond the refusal to acknowledge the reality of what's going on in one's body, and faced the dreadful sense of inhabiting an irrational and absurd world. Why does this happen to me? What's the sense of it?

This despair is particularly severe when one senses that one is a victim of injustice. If death and the pain of dying came only to those who were palpable sinners and reprobates then at least there would be a certain karma, or moral order in the universe. But Ilych feels that his life has been exemplary or, at least, basically correct. He has acted in conformity with the expectations of his superiors which is his norm for correct conduct. What is right is doing what your superiors would approve. This he has done, and in the light of that sense of moral rectitude (which, as he comes to discover, stems from a grievously inadequate moral standard) he feels that meaninglessness is aggravated by injustice. This is illustrated in the following:

> Ivan Ilych only waited till Gerasim had gone into the next room and then restrained himself no longer but wept like a child. He wept on account of his helplessness, his terrible loneliness, the cruelty of man, the cruelty of God, and the absence of God.

> "Why hast Thou done all this? Why hast Thou brought me here? Why, why dost Thou torment me so terribly?"

- 45 -

> He did not expect an answer and yet
> wept because there was no answer and
> could be none. The pain again grew more
> acute, but he did not stir and did not
> call. He said to himself: "Go on!
> Strike me! But what is it for? What
> have I done to Thee? What is it for?"
> (167)

This is a very poignant, a very trenchant,
expression of the sense of incoherence and cruelty in
the cosmos. Why death? And if death there has to be,
then, why me? I'm only 45, I've lived a basically good
life, I'm upright, why? It makes no sense. What is it
for? The feelings of meaninglessness and unjust
victimization aggravate the anxiety of dying and
death. This refrain occurs throughout the story.

> "Why these sufferings?" And the voice
> answered,

> "For no reason they just are so."
> Beyond and besides this there was
> nothing. (169)

> "Resistance is impossible!" he said to
> himself. "If I could only understand
> what it is all for! But that too is
> impossible. An explanation would be
> possible if it could be said that I have
> not lived as I ought to. But it is
> impossible to say that," and he
> remembered all the legality,
> correctitude and propriety of his life.
> "That at any rate can certainly not be
> admitted," he thought, and his lips
> smiled ironically as if someone could
> see that smile and be taken in by it.
> "There is no explanation! Agony, death
> ... What for?" (170)

Just as the torment of death is compounded by the
anxiety of meaninglessness, even so is it by the
anxiety of guilt. We have already had some intimations
of that. The anxiety of death can be complicated and
made more severe by the anxiety of guilt and
condemnation in one of two forms. One could say, for
example, what is happening to me is the just
consequences of my wickedness, of my wrong choices, of
my pursuit of selfish ends and neglect of justice.
Such a sense of guilt would go some way at least

towards resolving the meaninglessness described above. If the persons who suffer are the persons who sinned, they may experience guilt but they may continue to hold to some sense of coherence or fit in the universe between action and consequence.

But there is another more poignant kind of guilt. This is the pain of lost opportunity, the evaporation of time in which the past could be remedied in the light of values now clearly perceived through the prism of death as alone worthwhile. The virtues and joys of childhood and love, about which I want to say something in a moment, are examples of such positive values. If at the point of death one recognizes that the values so eagerly pursued and the kind of life that was lived were a delusion, a wrenching sense of guilt and despair seems inevitable. For now there no longer remains time in which to correct the error. This diffused sense of lost opportunity is perhaps the most severe of the causes of guilt and condemnation that assail persons at the end of their earthly pilgrimage. This is certainly the case with Ivan Ilych. For a long time he resists acknowledging that his life has in reality been anything but a life of moral rectitude. But as the hours pass he glimpses that he has grounded his self confidence about the correctness of his life on quicksand. He has in the main prized chimerical goods which in the harsh light of impending death are exposed as illusory.

> "And in imagination he began to recall the best moments of his pleasant life. But strange to say none of those best moments of his pleasant life now seemed at all what they had then seemed -- none of them except the first recollections of childhood. There, in childhood, there had been something really pleasant with which it would be possible to live if it could return. But the child that had experienced that happiness existed no longer, it was like a reminiscence of somebody else.
>
> As soon as the period began which had produced the present Ivan Ilych, all that had then seemed joys now melted before his sight and turned into something trivial and often nasty. And the further he departed from

childhood and the nearer he came to the present the more worthless and doubtful were the joys. This began with the School of Law. A little that was really good was still found there -- there was light-heartedness, friendship, and hope. But in the upper classes there had already been fewer of such good moments. Then during the first years of his official career, when he was in the service of the Governor, some pleasant moments again ocurred; they were the memories of love for a woman. Then all became confused and there was still less of what was good; later on again there was still less that was good, and the further he went the less there was. His marriage, a mere accident, then the disenchantment that followed it, a wife's bad breath and the sensuality and hypocrisy: then that deadly official life and those preoccupations about money, a year of it, and two, and ten, and twenty, and always the same thing. And the longer it lasted the more deadly it became, "It is as if I had been going downhill while I imagined I was going up. And that is really what it was. I was going up in public opinion, but to the same extent life was ebbing away from me. And now it is all done and there is only death." (168)

Tolstoy shows us the traumatic consciousness of lost opportunity when it appears that there no longer is time in which to remedy the failings of the past and strike a bargain to do better in the future. The growing perception that the way of life adopted was, in reality, trivial and nasty evokes a despairing guilt.

Perhaps enough has been said to show that the experience of dying and death is not an isolated experience, not something that can be pared away from the rest of life and its travails and dealt with by itself. Dying throws a spanner into our sense of the meaning of the universe, and it assails us with a strong sense of guilt, not only for particular actions which we wish we had not done, or actions not done which we wish we had, but also for the failure to use wisely and well the span of years that was given as a gift.

Tolstoy has supplied us a deeply incisive analysis of the consciousness of the dying person and the travail of soul that is induced by the prospect of the abyss. In the light of this, one would think that all persons would want to confront this anxiety-inducing demon, that they would want to wrestle with death and try to achieve some kind of victory over it. This is, in fact, what a large number of the religious traditions of the world are encouraging their adherents to do by one strategy or another. But there is -- as we have see -- another widespread response to death, and that is the response of denial. Just as Tolstoy gives us a penetrating analysis of the anxiety of dying and death, he also pares away the screens from human consciousness that prevent people from facing the reality of death. To illustrate with a celebrated passage:

> In the depth of his heart Ivan Ilych knew he was dying, but not only was he not accustomed to the thought, he simply did not and could not grasp it.
>
> The syllogism he had learned from Kiezewetter's Logic: "Caius is a man, men are mortal, therefore Caius is mortal," had always seemed to him correct as applied to Caius, but certainly not as applied to himself. That Caius -- man in the abstract -- was mortal, was perfectly correct, but he was not Caius, not an abstract man, but a creature quite, quite separate from all others. He had been little Vanya, with a mamma and a papa with Mitya and Voloya, with the toys, a coachman and a nurse, afterwards with Katenka and with all the joys, griefs, and delights of childhood, boyhood, and youth. What did Caius know of the smell of that striped leather ball Vanya had been so fond of? Had Caius kissed his mother's hand like that, and did the silk of her dress rustle so for Caius? Had he rioted like that at school when the pastry was bad? Had Caius been in love like that? Could Caius preside at a session as he did?" (154)

What a powerful presentation of the mechanism of denial! Of course, anyone knows that people are mortal even without the benefit of Kiezewetter's Logic! But this knowledge of human mortality is usually comprehended only with the top of one's head -- on the level of abstract logic -- and it is grasped more clearly with respect to the death of other people. The recognition of one's own personal vulnerability, finitude, and death, is so threatening that the mind tries vigorously to repress or deny this awareness. This evasion particularly characterises modern society, whose Promethean and hedonistic culture reinforces the universal, existential anxiety that inspires denial.

We turn to one other passage in which Tolstoy presents this denial of death:

> He could not understand it, and tried to drive this false, incorrect, morbid thought away and to replace it by other proper and healthy thoughts. But that thought, and not the thought only but the reality itself, seemed to confront him.
>
> And to replace that thought he called up a succession of others, hoping to find in them some support. He tried to get back into the former current of thoughts that had once screened the thoughts of death from him. But strange to say, all that had formerly shut off, hidden, and destroyed his consciousness of death no longer had that effect. Ivan Ilych now spent most of his time in attempting to re-establish that old current. (155)

What old current does Ivan Ilych seek to re-enter? It is the current of evasion, of screening, whereby the reality of his own death is comfortingly obscured because it is a terrifying prospect to face what death means. This is Ivan Ilych's state of thought and emotion until almost the end of his life.

Some readers are perplexed, even vexed, by the ending. Some critics have judged the analysis of the consciousness of dying and death, the psychic mechanisms of evasion, the psychology of sickness, to be brilliantly done, but think Tolstoy is injecting a discordant special pleading at the end. They feel that the ending does not resonate realistically with the brilliant analysis that has gone before. Whether or not the denouement is consistent with the preceding disclosure of Ivan Ilych's life will of course, remain a subjective judgement. I wish, however, to share a few thoughts about that conclusion.

The ultimate answer that transforms the pain and perplexity of death into acceptance and triumph comes to Ivan Ilych two hours before his death. Just prior to the advent of that answer, he personifies the typical first reaction to death, namely, terror and resistance. His unresolved doubts about the meaning of this horrible and painful experience, and his scream of resistance "I won't" -- continued by the prolonged screaming of the letter O -- as he struggles against being thrust into the black sack of death, bear witness to the destructive power of death. Tolstoy reveals the paradox of death in portraying the dialectical character of Ivan Ilych's agony. ('Dialectical' simply means to say 'yes' and 'no' simultaneously.) On the one hand, Ivan Ilych struggles against his total enclosure in death's black sack; on the other, he is tormented even more by his inability to let go and get right into it. What prevents his acceptance of death is his conviction that his life had been a good one and his suffering and death, therefore, cruelly unwarranted. This inability to see his life in its true dimensions, his tenacity in clinging to deceptions about himself, the drive to continue to think well of himself, in a word, this self-justification continues almost to the end, and comes near to preventing an honest confrontation with death.

The transformation when it finally comes, comes in the form of the touch of his son's head and lips upon his hand. "His schoolboy son had crept softly in to the bedroom and gone up to the bedside. The dying man was still screaming desperately and waving his arms; his hand fell on the boy's head and the boy caught it pressed it to his lips and began to cry. At that very moment, Ivan Ilych fell through and caught sight of the light." (174) Two truths came home to Ivan Ilych. The first is that his life had not been what it should have been. The honest acknowledgment of the trivality and the self-centredness of much, perhaps most, of his adult years bestows the release for which he had been yearning. This brutal act of honesty with himself finally enables him to see the quality of his life for what it had been -- basically selfish, trivial and, at times, nasty. That is the first truth that comes home to him: the need to see oneself truly.

But if repentance is the first step, the discovery of love is the second. In the light of his confession of waste and failure, he asks, "What is the right thing?" In effect, he declares, "I acknowledge that I have botched things horribly, that my life has been a delusion of false values, vain pursuits, trivial preoccupations and plain selfishness. I see it now -- but what is it that I should have done?" The disclosure comes when he feels his son kissing his hand. In the act of receiving compassion, he learns also how to give it. He opens his eyes and seeing his desolate son, feels sorry for him, as for his wife who then approaches the bed. With his last breath he murmurs his sorrow for the pain he caused them and his lips do not quite finish framing the appeal for forgiveness that this heart utters.

His final thoughts require some explanation, especially since at fist glance they seem to contradict the claim I have been labouring to make that death is a source of universal anxiety. We read: "There was no fear because there was no death." (175) His last words to himself were "Death is finished" ... It is no more!" An important point to be noted is that the words 'It is finished' are words of Jesus spoken from the cross. The point of the story will not be fully grasped unless it is recognized that Tolstoy is writing out of an intensly Christian background at this point in his life. Consequently the images, the nuances, are now shaped by his own profound conversion experience. Tolstoy places Ivan Ilych's redemption from sin and death in the context of the Christian message of God's saving work accomplished through the crucifixion and resurrection of Christ. The words, 'It is finished', convey an answer to death which is implied rather than stated. But this is an implication which would be grasped only by those who know the code, who recognize that phrase as the words of Jesus spoken from what Christians regard as the life-transforming, death-destroying cross. Quite obviously, the claim that death does not exist, is, in a straightforward sense, false. Death is not finished; the inevitable prospect remains that we shall all die. What has changed is the meaning of the experience of death. Before his discovery of the truth about himself and about life's highest value -- love; that is, before his conversion, Ivan Ilych was terrified by death.

Subsequent to his acceptance of light, of the transforming revelation of grace and love, the fear of death is vanquished.

Interpretations of death need to distinguish between the primordial or raw experience of death which religious traditions and existential anthropology characterize as terror and absurdity, and the revised assessments, induced by religious traditions, in which death is deprived of ultimate threat. Accordingly, this testimony at the end of Ivan Ilych's life that death is finished, should not be misunderstood as a refutation of my initial thesis that death is an existential anxiety to which religious traditions seek to give a therapeutic answer or, alternatively, that is otherwise repressed and denied. Rather than being a refutation of that premise, it is a confirmation of it. We have seen throughout, Ivan Ilych's instinctive reaction to death. He concedes Caius' mortality, but not his own; and with good reason, for he fears death and does not want to die. At the end, where we find this affirmation that there is no fear because there is no death, we encounter the response of a person upon whom a religious tradition has done its transformative work. Perhaps the matter should be understood more concretely: we encounter the response of someone upon whom grace, kindness and love have done their work. The grace of Gerasim, the serving boy; the pathetic grace, love and devotion of the son who barely understands what is transpiring, have transformed Ivan Ilych. And in the light of that human transformation, the response to death also undergoes transmutation.

REFERENCES

Tolstoy, Leo
"The Death of Ivan Ilych." This brilliant
and poignant story has been widely
anthologized. The pagination in my text
refers to Irving Howe, ed., Classics of
Modern Fiction: Eight Short Novels. New
York: Harcourt, Brace & World, 1968.

CHAPTER FOUR

THE RESPONSE OF IMMORTALITY OF
THE SOUL IN HINDU TRADITION

1. The Dialogue of Arjuna and Krishna in the Bhagavad
   Gita

In our earlier confirmation of the universal dread
of death, we looked briefly at the Bhagavad Gita's
account of the exchange that takes place between Arjuna
of the Pandavas and his charioteer on the eve of the
momentous battle with the Kauravas for dynastic
supremacy. We noted the desolation of spirit induced
in Arjuna by his contemplation of the ensuing slaughter
and the declaration of his intention to desist from the
battle. His charioteer intrudes upon this scene of
dismay with a message that has powerfully moulded the
course of Indian religious thought and experience. The
charioteer who gives the therapeutic, transformative
message to the desolate Arjuna is none other than the
Lord, temporarily in incognito form.[1]

Lord Krishna, in popular Hindu iconography, is
typically shown holding his flute, whose beautiful
music enchants the gopis or cow-herdesses. One such is
Radha who establishes a particular relationship with
Krishna and is frequently depicted as Lord Krishna's
consort in Hindu iconography and painting. The
characteristic blue hue to Krishna's face suggests that
the worship of Lord Krishna is the result of the
assimilation into Hinduism of a local cult, perhaps
Dravidian, that existed in India prior to the advent of
the Aryan invaders in roughly 1500 B.C. The Aryan
religious tradition, whose beliefs and way of life are
reflected in the literature known as the Vedas,
expanded into what subsequently was called Hinduism,
'Hindu' being the Persian word for the dwellers of the
land beyond the Indus. This expansion entailed the
incorporation into Aryan or vedic religion of some
local religious traditions, one of which, so the
scholarly supposition goes, was the cult of Lord
Krishna. With his dark blue hue Krishna betrays his
provenance from indigenous dark skinned Dravidian
people.

It is this divine being, Krishna, who engages in a
dialogue with Arjuna (who has shown apprehension at
fighting and killing), and gives him encouragement. It
is very important not to confuse the truly therapeutic,

transformative, or salvific answer of the _Gita_ with
another doctrine that is very prominent in Indian
thought, and that is the doctrine of rebirth (_samsara_).
It might be commonly thought that to assert the reality
of reincarnation, or rebirth, is sufficient to abolish
or mitigate the apprehension of death.   On this
mistaken view, the devotee is told, in effect, "Don't
worry, you'll be reincarnated", the presumption being
that this assurance would provide an adequate therapy
for death anxiety.   This is not so in the _Gita_ nor
Indian   thought   generally,   though   belief   in
reincarnation may function therapeutically in some
other culture-contexts in dealing with the pain and
problem of death.

        I am informed that the Tsimshan Indians on the
west coast of Canada, also hold a doctrine of
reincarnation.   The anxiety of death seems under
control among the Tsimshan, in part because among them
the doctrine of rebirth does have an assuaging or
mitigating power.   Accordingly, I would not want to
generalize   from   the   classical   Indian   view   of
transmigration to all cultures that hold a similar
doctrine.   But it is certainly true of the Hindu
context now under discussion that the doctrine of
rebirth rather than being an answer to death, points to
dimensions of the problem, in that the cycles of the
soul's transmigration are experienced as bondage, as a
tedious burden, from which deliverance is sought.
Perhaps reincarnation is experienced as bondage rather
than deliverance because the Hindu time span is so
vast.

        Even if the soul freed at death from its
incarceration in the gross or physical body should
enter some celestial abode, this should not be taken as
evidence of ultimate deliverance from the phenomenal
realm of _samsara_, where birth, death and rebirth (and
redeath) hold sway.   For such a celestial post-death
state would be only an interlude before the soul --
driven by the karmic determinants imprinted upon its
subtle body -- adopts once more a gross body and
reenters the pain and ignorance of worldly, samsaric
existence.   Only knowledge of the true self and
consequent liberation (_moksha_) from the weary and
sorrowful round of rebirth and redeath can be
understood as an adequate response to death.

        To return to the Gita's story: the first argument
that Lord Krishna uses is that fighting is Arjuna's

duty. He ought not to be concerned about the consequences of the impending slaughter; his sole responsibility is to perform his duty. Better one's own duty poorly done, than somebody else's duty well done. Duty, in this context, means basically the performance of caste obligations. Since Arjuna is a member of the warrior class, the kshatriya caste, it is his duty to engage in the battle without taking account of consequences. This first argument employed by Krishna in the face of Arjuna's reluctance to engage in the battle could, in itself, provide for some people a therapy for the anxiety of death. One ought not to concern oneself with the consequences, either in one's own life or in someone else's, of a particular course of action. In life, one is given an assignment; one does one's duty, maintains honour, acts with decency, with nobility, with justice, and has no regard for any deleterious or unpleasant results. I doubt that this is a great source of solace to a large number of people nowadays; but it may well be that in another time the fulfillment of duty -- obedience to social and transcendent demands -- was sufficient to assuage the anxiety of death. This answer, however, is not where we want to put our stress; attention is drawn to it simply in passing.

The second argument that Lord Krishna advances towards Arjuna is that if he does not fight, he will incur shame. His fellow warriors will think that he is reluctant to fight out of cowardice, with the result that his good reputation will be destroyed. This is also an argument that does not particularly concern our present investigation and we shall, therefore, pass it by and look, instead, at the third and most important argument.

2.   The Spiritual Nature of the True Self

If rebirth (which is simply taken for granted as the most suitable explanation for the apparent inequities of life) is not the answer to the pain and perplexity of death, what is? Lord Krishna's decisive message to Arjuna is that it is the doctrine of the immortal soul. It is foolish of Arjuna to be preoccupied and anxious about death because the real self cannot die.

This doctrine presupposes what Franklin Edgerton, whose exposition of the Gita I largely follow here, calls anthropological dualism. The Gita's analysis of what it means to be human is dualistic, meaning that the empirically observed human being has two dimensions. This twofold nature is designated by two Sanskrit words. On the one side, there is purusha, or atman, which we may call the soul, or self, provided the qualifier 'true' or 'real' is understood before the terms self or soul. In addition to purusha there is another component rendered in Sanskrit as prakriti which we may roughly translate for our purpose as matter.

For those who might wish to explore these matters a little more deeply, I shall indicate three other related concepts. Prakriti is made up of three ingredients: sattva, rajas, and tamas. Sattva we may render as purity or goodness; rajas as passion or activity; and tamas as darkness, heaviness or laziness. All material things are combined, in varying degrees, of these three elements. The nature of a thing is determined by the degree to which one ingredient predominates over the others. In certain Eastern dietetic disciplines, food is selected in terms of its degree of sattva over against how much tamas or rajas it has. Because the body is the consequence of what is eaten, food with an excess of the tamas component will make the body itself tamasic or heavy in quality. Similarly, rajasic food will make the body excessively active and turbulent. Accordingly, foods that are characterized by the quality satva (lightness or goodness) should preponderate in the diet.

The important thing to grasp here is that a radical differentiation is made between these two modes of existence: between purusha or the spirit element, on the one hand, and prakriti or the material element, on the other. It is this metaphysical differentiation that underlies the answer to the dilemmas and vicissitudes of history, including death. For death is something that occurs only on the level of prakriti or matter. What happens in space and time -- pain, travail, sufferings and anxieties -- does not touch the real self. The real self, ultimately and essentially, is utterly separated from the arena in which these deleterious things take place. Sickness, decrepitude, and death are, for the Gita, real enough, but they occur only on the profane, untransformed level of samsaric existence. These events happen only to the material component of personality: they do not touch the real self.[2]

It should be understood that prakriti, which has been loosely designated as material existence, is not what is commonly understood by 'matter'. If the properties of prakriti and purusha (which we designate spirit or the real self) were placed in parallel columns, it would be a serious mistake to subsume under prakriti only bare material existence. For on the side of prakriti would go many of the qualities that are frequently regarded as mental qualities, such as imagining, reasoning, and feeling. Aspects of consciousness that one might be tempted to put on the spiritual side belong, in this Hindu analysis, to the matter side.

Clues are given to this effect when the atman or self is described as unmanifest and inconceivable. This implies that qualities like imagining, feeling, sensing, conceiving, cannot be the real self, for the real self is transcendent -- is beyond all our normal experience. In sum, it must be borne in mind that the purusha/prakriti distinction should not be construed in terms of the conventional Western mind/body dichotomy, since prakriti includes much of what is there meant by mind.

The Gita's anthropological dualism should not, moreover, be confused with the teachings of other Hindu philosophers such as Shankara. Shankara is a ninth century A.D. Indian philosopher who receives the major credit for formulating a philosophic position called advaita vedanta, which is probably the best known of the various Hindu schools in the west. The advaita vedanta not only makes a radical differentiation between the spiritual and material elements but goes on to say that, in the last analysis, the material element does not exist. There is a great deal of subtlety and complexity into which we cannot go in the present context. I stress the words 'in the last analysis' because the material realm does have, as the expositors say, a relative reality, so long as one lives in a state of ignorance. Until enlightenment is reached, the material world of things and body, society and history, simply must be taken into account. But when moksha -- spiritual enlightenment and release -- which is the ultimate goal of existence is attained, then the realm of prakriti is seen as basically unreal. The world becomes maya, signifying illusory existence. The Gita, in contradistinction, does not assert that the world of material things including bodily existence is unreal. The Gita does not go in as extreme a spiritual direction as does Shankara. It affirms the reality of prakriti, but insists that it is not the true self. The body exists but it must not be confused with the essential self which is spirit.

A further claim made by the advaita vedanta is that atman, or soul, when properly understood, is identical to the absolute spiritual reality, the Brahman. This is conveyed by the epigram tat tvam asi, "that thou art". This means that the real spiritual self, the atman, is the invisible, spiritual, essential reality of the universe, Brahman, God, the absolute. It is not so much a matter of becoming the Brahman -- the way a drop of water flows into the sea and becomes one with the sea. Rather, it is a matter of reaching the stage of enlightenment where the knowledge that one already is and always was the Brahman becomes palpable.

Attention has been drawn to two differentiations between the advaita and the Gita's teaching. Both share the conviction about the nature of the true self as totally differentiated from matter. Shankara and the advaita go on to say that, in the last analysis, matter is unreal. Furthermore, for Shankara, the self is identical with God, while for the Gita it is not. The Gita insists on the separate reality of the soul. It resists the direction in which Shankara went, in which the metaphysical identity of self and Brahman, is asserted.

The reason for this difference between the Gita and Shankara is the diverse conceptions of God with which they operate. For Shankara, God, Brahman, is an impersonal force, having neither attributes nor personality. Brahman is without name and form (Sanskrit nama-rupa). God is utterly transcendent and nothing said about God taken from human experience of distinctions would be appropriate. Any predications about God would ultimately be false.

For the Gita, God is a supremely personal being, towards whom the proper relationship is one of love. Love is relational process that presupposes two autonomous centres of personality. The lover cannot totally assimilate the beloved. In the relation of love there can be deep communion, but it is a union of moral wills. This is quite different from the metaphysical identity of the impersonal God and self which Shankara propounds. Though the Gita does not exclude this monistic interpretation, it regards the idea of God as an impersonal being without attributes, as a lower understanding of divinity. God, fully and truly understood, is a personal being who comes down to earth to succour humankind, sings songs that delight the devotees, and with flowers in hand and serene smile on lips, bestows peace and blessing upon them. Because the Gita understands the relationship of God to humans to be one of personal intimacy, ecstasy, love -- in a word, because of its theism -- it must insist that the self is not identical with God. Otherwise, there would be no relationship of love. There might be absorption or identity, but there would be no loving devotee giving praise, devotion, and faith to God. Conversely, there would be no loving God giving his/her grace, kindness, and mercy to the devotee. In order for there to be the relationship of love, the self, the atman, must remain distinct from God. As one Hindu sage of the bhakti or devotional school said, "I want to taste sugar, not become sugar."

In spite of these differences, the advaita and the Gita along with the Sankhya and yoga philosophies, share this basic point of departure: the spiritual nature of the self. In the passages of the Gita which here concern us, the character of spirit is elaborated. The real self, as spirit, is totally invulnerable to what happens in space and time. Destruction of this imperishable one, the atman, no one can cause. In their famous dialogue, Lord Krishna instructs Arjuna on the nature of the self:

19. Who believes him [the atman] a slayer,
    And who thinks him slain,
    Both these understand not:
    He slays not, is not slain.

20. He is not born, nor does he ever die;
    Nor having come to be, will he ever more
    come not to be.
    Unborn, eternal everlasting, this
    ancient one [the atman]
    Is not slain when the body is slain.

21. Who knows as indestructible and eternal
    This unborn, imperishable one,
    That man son of Prtha, [Arjuna], how
    Can he slay, or cause to slay -- whom?

22. As leaving aside worn-out garments
    A man takes other, new ones,

so leaving aside worn-out bodies
To other, new ones goes the embodied
(soul).

23. Swords cut him not,
    Fire burns him not,
    Water wets him not,
    Wind dries him not.

24 Not to be cut is he, not to be burnt is
    he,
    Not be be wet nor yet dried
    Eternal, omnipresent, fixed,
    Immovable, everlasting is he.

25 Unmanifest he, unthinkable he,
    Unchangeable he is declared to be;
    Therefore knowing him thus
    Thou shouldst not mourn him.

This teaching about the self is the first phase of the Gita's central therapeutic message. Confronted by death, understand who you are, understand your essential nature as a spiritual being. In our space/time world, change is constant; both cellular and psychic life have changed since this enquiry was started. There is, however, one thing that remains untouched and changes not -- that is the atman. The self is indestructible and eternal. The self is not implicated in material, historical and social events. The true self is totally detached from worldly events. Shortly before this was written I went into a political campaign office. A lot of people were scurrying around, examining voters' lists, making up signs, getting ready to go out to canvas, and so on. On the Gita's analysis, this activity is something in which the real self has no interest, for it is utterly detached from it. Such worldly aims may be pursued, if they are one's duty, but the real self, as such, does not engage in them. Prakriti -- the material or phenomenal personality -- may be furious, frantic and fanatical in the pursuit of these historical, political, economic, social, material, biological activities. The real self remains immovable, imperishable, unmanifest.

Finally, the self is unthinkable. In the last analysis this kind of language employed to characterize the self is a flimsy and failing effort. Because the self is so different from our ordinary experience it cannot be captured in a conceptual net. Efforts may be made, but the stress in the Indic tradition falls on experiencing the self, not describing the self. Ultimately the self so transcends our routine existence that we cannot adequately conceptualize its nature; hence the stress on directly intuiting the self.

3. Three Ways of Liberating The Self

The question now emerges as to the way in which one comes to know this mysterious, ineffable self whose discovery would mean freedom from finitude and fear. The theoretical acknowledgement of the immortal atman or self is only the first stage of the Gita's answer to the pain and problematic of death; a second stage is clearly necessary. The fact of the matter is that most people do not truly know the real self. They persist in living as though their mental and biological dimensions were their real self. Obviously something has gone wrong in human life and the Gita is quite clear what it is. The trouble is traced back to a process of entanglement, in which the proximity of the true spiritual self, purusha, to material, psychological prakriti has caused a metaphysical confusion or ignorance of the real self.

Immediately a certain problem has to be anticipated; how can this marvellous and mysterious imperishable self make that kind of mistake? In religious traditions there are a number of premises that go unchallenged and are simply accepted as axiomatic. One of these is that because of the proximity of matter to spirit such confusions and entanglements take place. Consequently such deluded persons develop what the Gita calls the I-faculty in which the self is identified with the psychological and material aspects of personality. They experience cravings which aim at the satisfaction of psychological drives and needs and material wants, and then suppose this desiring ego is the real self. Clearly a process is required that effects the disengagement of the real self from delusive material existence.

The question is how is this done; how does one come to a transforming knowledge of the real self? How can the transcendent self escape its bondage to the wheel of rebirth and redeath which results from the self's encapsulation in the body and its resultant deluded enmeshment with matter? It is the genius of the Gita to have synthesized three different ways, corresponding to three different personality types, and it is probably for this reason that it is so enormously influential in Indian thought.

The Gita affirms that the realization of the true self which is invulnerable to the pain and perplexity of death can be achieved, in the first place, through knowledge. (The Sanskrit term for this way of knowledge is jnana marga). This way entails the kind of activity that is conducted by a yogin, i.e., an ascetic, who practices austerities and meditates so that the appetites of the body and the distractions of the mind are, over a period of time, subdued and eventually eliminated. By thus stilling the claims of the body through yogic postures (asanas), and the agitations of the mind through meditation, the yogin attains a single-mindedness or one-pointedness that allows him to perceive the true self. An image frequently used is that the self is revealed like a pebble at the bottom of a stilled pool of water.

This way of self-realization through mystical knowledge is advocated by Shankara in his philosophy of advaita vedanta. The precondition of this spiritual knowledge is the adoption of the life of a renunciant (sanyassin), rejecting the pursuit of pleasure, material possessions, and even family claims and social obligations. Only by thus divesting oneself of all competing concerns that would distract from the pursuit of mystic trance, can knowledge of the self be attained. For Shankara the knowledge of the self would also be knowledge of the Brahman -- the invisible, transcendent essence which is identical with the self. The Gita acknowledges the legitimacy of the way of knowledge but is not enthralled by it as a normative way. The Blessed One, Krishna, informs Arjuna:

"Renunciation and discipline of action
both lead to supreme weal.
But of these two, rather than
renunciation of action,
Discipline of action is superior." (V,2)

The Gita recognizes that renunciation and knowledge do lead, like disciplined action, to supreme weal, that is, the highest good of liberation of the self from the wheel of karma-samsara. But of these two, discipline of action is better. The Gita sounds this theme on numerous occasions:

"The man of discipline [that is, the man
who is engaged in his community] is
higher than men of austerities,
Also than men of knowledge he is held to
be higher;
And the man of discipline is higher than
men of ritual action;
Therefore be a man of discipline,
Arjuna." (VI, 46)

Disciplined action -- the way of karma yoga -- is
higher than austerities and meditations of the yoga of
knowledge that induce the mystic trance of samhadi in
which the essential self is experienced.

The problem that the Gita is trying to deal with
here is the reconciliation of action and liberation.
The premise which appears constant throughout all the
competing and diverse schools of Indian thought is
karma -- the conviction that action leads irrevocably
to reaction. As a man sows that shall be reap; there
are no arbitrary results. Everything that happens,
happens according to a cosmic pattern, a law of moral
determinism. The implications of the law of karma
seem, at first glance, dismaying. As long as one acts,
even if one does good deeds, one is still involved in
reaction and, therefore, rebirth. How then, since
action seems inescapable, is one to achieve deliverance
from this cycle of rebirth in which suffering and death
take place? It was in response to this problem that
the exponents of the way of knowledge argued that the
only way to break the dreary cycle of rebirth is to
stop acting, to withdraw from society, to minimize
action as far as one could and to concentrate on the
realization of the self through austerity and
meditation.

The Gita, on the contrary, says that not to act
is, for most people, impossible. However, there is a
way out of this dilemma; that is to act in a particular
way. This means, first of all, to do one's duty. Duty
is understood as the performance of one's dharma --
those social rules that are applicable to a person's
stage in life and particularly his caste or social
class. But in order to achieve release one's duty must
be done with a special attitude. Duty must be done
without thought to the consequences, in abstract
obedience to the social rules without calculating the
diverse results of alternative courses of action. Nor
need practitioners be plagued with anxiety about the

precise nature of what they should do, for this is laid down in the <u>Dharma Shastras</u> or law books which elaborate the obligations of the members of society. One should not emulate Arjuna, who, before Krishna delivered the therapeutic message which led to his enlightenment, was agitated about the consequences of the battle. All that Arjuna needed to do was his caste duty without attachment to the fruits or consequences of his action.

This insight is one of the greatest legacies of the <u>Gita</u> to Indian life. One important way to the highest good (understood as the self's deliverance from the samsaric realm of ignorance and rebirth) advocates social action. Contrary to what the advocates of knowledge -- the renunciants or men of austerity -- say, one can still act in this life, can still be engaged in the social, political, and historical life of one's community, and attain to spiritual deliverance, provided such action is in the <u>Gita's</u> spirit of detachment.

Let us look at some textual support for this teaching of action without attachment. Many passages could be isolated but we shall restrict ourselves to one rather long one which puts the matter very well.

"All whose undertakings
Are free from desire and purpose,
His actions burnt up in the fire of knowledge,
Him the wise called the man of learning.

Abandoning attachment to the fruits of action,
Constantly content, independent,
Even when he sets out upon action,
He yet does (in effect) nothing whatsoever." (IV, 19-20)

The person characterized in the foregoing is acting, but the result, as far as pertains to karmic determinism and rebirth, is the same as if he had done nothing. How is this so? Because his action is done without attachment to the fruits of the action, the consequences. His caste duty stipulates fighting and he fights, or tanning leathers and he tans, or carrying garbage and he acquiesces, or teaching the vedas and he teaches. By simply doing his duty without attachment to the results, the self is freed from enmeshment in

matter and revealed in its purity and autonomy. The
soul's transcendence of all historical, social, and
material involvement, is very trenchantly brought out
in the following verse:

"Free from wishes, with mind and soul
    restrained,
Abandoning all possessions,
Action with the body alone,
Performing, he attains no guilt."

What can "action with the body alone performing"
possibly mean? With this assertion the Gita testifies
that such detached action is done only by matter, and
not by the true, transcendent self. Because the action
is done without any involvement, without any
psychological or emotional investment in what is going
to happen, the soul remains quite separate from the
action. Therefore, it does not accumulate karma which,
in turn, would dictate further rebirths.

The reality of an utterly autonomous soul, beyond
all ordinary human experience and historical
determinism is reiterated in various ways.

"Content with getting what comes by
    chance,
Passed beyond the pairs (of opposites),
    free from jealousy,
Indifferent to success and failure,
Even acting, he is not bound." (IV, 22)

The important phrase for our purpose is, "Even
acting he is not bound". Such an actor is not bound by
karma to the wheel of birth.

"Rid of attachment, freed, ... his
    action all melts away." (IV, 23)

What that means is all his karma melts away. In other
words, action done in this particular way, does not
accumulate karma. One is no longer bound into that
cause and effect nexus that binds humans into this
mundane vale of tears.

One way of doing actions without attachment to
their fruits, is by doing it as an offering to God. if
difficulty is experienced in doing actions with a sense
of indifference to their results, one should try
offering one's deeds to God.

Casting all actions upon Brahman
Whoso acts abandoning attachment,
Evil does not cleave to him
As water (does not cleave) to a
  lotus-leaf. (V, 10)

"If thou hast no ability even for
  practice,
[if you are not good at karma marga]
Be wholly devoted to work for Me;
[Lord Krishna -- for God]
For My sake also actions
Performing, thou shalt win perfection."
(XII, 10)

A technique for disinterested actions is to do them as
a service or offering to God, and to remain unconcerned
with whatever happens subsequently.

The third way of spiritual emancipation
promulgated by the Gita is the way of devotion --
bhakti marga or bhakti yoga. (Bhakti means devotion).
The Gita satisfies philosophers; it ministers to the
followers of dharma, the social activists, as long as
they are engaged without attachment to results. But
the Gita's preferred way is the way of devotion. This
is the great secret of the Gita which some scholars
claim gave a decisive skewing to the development of
Hinduism. Thereafter, Hinduism was pushed in the
direction of theism, that is, belief in, and adoration
of, a personal supreme being. In the Upanishads -- at
least those focussed upon by Shankara -- one discovers
the predominance of the monistic viewpoint that
Shankara developed into the advaita vedanta
philosophy. Had that strand of religiosity prevailed,
then the central form of Hindu piety would have been
focussed on an impersonal, indescribable essence --
Brahman -- about which nothing should ultimately be
said since all predication would be false. But
principally because of the Gita a decisive impulse in
the direction of theistic religion was given to the
Hindu tradition. The Gita proposes that the easiest
and best way to achieve the self's liberation from the
world of prakriti (matter), the world of maya
(illusion) and samsara (rebirth) is by single-minded
love, faith and devotion to God.

"Further, the highest secret of all,
My supreme message, hear.
Because thou art greatly loved of Me,

Therefore I shall tell thee what is good
for thee.

Be Me-minded, devoted to Me;
Worshipping Me, revere Me;
And to Me alone shalt thou go; truly to
thee
I promise it -- (because) thou art dear
to Me.

Abandoning all (other) duties,
Go to Me as thy sole refuge;
From all evils I thee
Shall rescue; be not grieved!
(XVIII, 64-66)

This is the Gita's highest secret: there is a way
of liberation from this weary round where pain,
sickness, decrepitude, and death take place and that is
by overflowing love for God. By devotion to Lord
Krishna -- the incarnation of God -- and by receiving
his love, deliverance is granted from the weary tedium
of rebirth of a phenomenal ego misperceived as the
essential self. What cannot be done by austerity, or
by disciplined action, God does as an act of grace, an
act of kindness. Those who are Christians should find
this a familiar psychological ambience. This is the
religious context of a God who loves his devotees and
delivers them from all suffering, failure, and death.

To sum up: the Gita's therapy exists on two
levels. First, it calls for a recognition of the true
nature of the self as immortal, invisible,
imperishable, transcendent atman or soul. Some might
have thought that an instructive analysis of the self
would, in itself, provide the therapy for ignorance and
death. On this assumption, the transformative message
would consist of a reminder that whatever mortal ills
may come, they are not being visited upon the real self
but to an ephemeral material being. But inasmuch as it
is so difficult for people to recognize the true self
-- because of the entanglement of the spiritual self
with matter -- the Gita then specifies three modalities
of liberation: the way of knowledge, which it approves
but does not think highly of; the way of disciplined
action, which it esteems a great deal more; and
ultimately the way of devotion, which is its preeminent
solution to human plight.

NOTES

1. Edgerton sketches the scene as follows:
    "In form, it consists mainly of a long dialog,
    which is almost a monolog. The principal speaker
    is Kṛṣṇa, who in human aspect is merely one of the
    secondary heroes of the Mahābhārata, the great
    Hindu epic. but, according to the Gītā itself, he
    is in truth a manifestation of the Supreme Deity
    in Human form. Hence the name -- the Song (gītā)
    of the Blessed One or the Lord (Bhagavad). The
    other speaker in the dialog is Arjuna, one of the
    sons of Pāṇḍu who are the principal heroes of the
    Mahābhārata." (Edgerton 1964: 105).

2. Cf., "The soul [purusha] is absolutely unitary,
    undifferentiated, and without qualities; not
    subject to any change or alteration, and not
    participating in any action. Material nature, or
    the non-soul, is what performs acts. It assumes
    manifold forms and is constantly subject to change
    -- evolution, devolution, and variation".
    (Edgerton 1964: 140-1).

REFERENCES

Edgerton, Franklin.
     1964 The Bhagavad Gita. New York: Harper & Row
          (Torchbooks). Comprises translation and
          interpretation.

CHAPTER FIVE

SURVIVAL IN HEBRAIC TRADITION

1. The Assessment of Death in the Hebrew Scriptures:
Existential Despair or Serene Acceptance?

I have conducted this exploration of death and
afterlife on the premise that death induces a profound
existential anxiety to which the religious traditions
respond, in various ways, with a 'coping mechanism' or
therapeutic strategy. But do the Hebrew Scriptures, in
fact, view death as terror and a problem with which
they must deal?

The conventional judgement has been affirmative.
Death -- the loss of life-force and the fate of Sheol
-- is viewed with anxiety; it is something one wishes
to avoid. For death means separation, first, from the
community which gives identity and meaning to the
individual and, second, from God himself. "In death
there is no rememberance of thee, in Sheol who can give
thee praise?" (Palms 6:5)

A challenge to the view that the Old Testament
exemplifies this understanding of death as threat is
offered by Lloyd Bailey in Biblical Perspectives on
Death. He argues that apart from a narrow stratum of
late literature (notably the Book of Daniel) that
represents a shift from the normative and dominant Old
Testament view to an apocalyptic eschatology, the Old
Testament confronts death in an unagitated and
accepting way. The reason for this serenity is the Old
Testament's understanding of death as a natural process
consistent with the original will of God in
creation.[1]

Such distress about death as does appear in the
Old Testament pertains not to death as an existential
human condition, but to certain unfortunate conditions
of death. Bailey lists the conditions that make for a
"bad" death: it may be premature; it may be violent;
it may leave no surviving heir. He then enumerates the
conditions of a 'good' death which are the opposite of
the conditions of a 'bad' death. A good or timely
death comes peacefully at the end of the long life
leaving progeny to carry on one's memory and name.

Bailey's interpretation of the Old Testament's
perspective on death is amplified somewhat by his

discrimination between two strands in the Genesis myth which he terms 'folk explanations' of death.

(1) The first sees death as an intruder upon human paradisal bliss, an intrusion precipitated by the sin of pride. Without sin, humanity would have been immortal.

(2) The second view sees death as a natural outcome of mankind's creation out of clay. Because man, like the animals, is fashioned out of clay, he must, like the animals, return to the ground in death. Thus death is both natural and acceptable.

Bailey argues that though the first view (death as punishment) became central in Christian thought it played no role in subsequent Old Testament literature and a very small role in Rabbinic literature. The intent of these arguments is to demonstrate that death, as such, is not viewed as an absurd enemy, but only its untimeliness. When death occurs at the right time, in the appropriate condition, then it is not only natural but also a friend. But there are some problems or inadequacies in Bailey's thesis.

(a) <u>Logically unwarranted inferences</u>

First, and most briefly, the arbitrary nature of some of the extrapolations from the Genesis story of creation must be noted. These extrapolations which constitute the second or 'natural' explanation of death rest, in fact, on two non-sequiturs. The assumption that creation from clay signifies mortality may be countered with the claim that when inspired by the divine Spirit clay may, indeed, become immortal -- apart from the effects of sin.

The second assumption that the kinship of man with the animals signifies mortality, begs the question whether the animals -- again, apart from the ecological ramifications of human sin -- were also intended to be immortal.

So far we have left aside the question whether the inferences contained in the second (natural) etiology of death are drawn by Bailey or by the Old Testament writers themselves. Whether these authors are as

sanguine about death as Bailey, however, is a doubt
raised by assertions he himself makes; for example:

> "To be sure, this explanation [death as
> natural] has been merged with the one
> previously discussed, so that as the entire
> chapter now stands, the statement about
> returning to dust appears to be punishment, to
> be a fate not intended for the humans."
> (Bailey 1979: 38)

If the canonical understanding of death is that
evinced by the completed text as just indicated, I am
perplexed how the claim can be made that "mortality as
the Creator's design for humans seems to be the basic
perspective of the Old Testament literature ...."
(Bailey 1979: 38)

(b) Ineluctable 'Untimeliness' of Death

The second reservation about Bailey's argument is
that it assumes that the Old Testament ignores one of
the most distressing traits of death that gives it its
power to instill terror. I mean its unpredictability.
Since death can strike at any moment, and not only when
we are aged and weary and our work done, it can never
be deprived of its terror. Even if we are ripe in
years and accomplishments, we still fear for our
children: will they survive the capricious
possibilities of death?

In a sense, all or most death is 'bad' death which
makes us anxious, inasmuch as we can experience
proleptically the termination of our human relations
and creative tasks long before we are prepared to
relinquish them. Even if with good luck some of us
should arrive at a 'good' death at the end, we should
have lived a great deal of our life in terror and
apprehension that a bad, i.e., untimely, death might
strike us or our loved ones down.

The same hermeneutical problem that we noted in
the first objection emerges here. Is the failure (on
my premises) to acknowledge the unpredictable and
proleptic quality of death Bailey's or that of the Old
Testament authors? Is Bailey simply the careful
describer of the Old Testament's view (regardless of
what judgement we might subsequently wish to make upon
it) or has his procedure, in fact, entailed a
misleading interpretation of selected passages? In the

light of his shortcomings in dealing with the distinction to which I now turn, it is reasonable to postulate that the Old Testament, rather than expressing a serene acceptance of the naturalness of death, shares a near universal apprehension about it that calls forth a consoling response.

(c)   Initial vs. Transformed Interpretations of Death

The major weakness of Bailey's analysis of the biblical view of death is its failure to distinguish clearly between an existential attitude (in which death may be understood as pain and problem) and a soteriologically transformed attitude in which the experience and meaning of death is altered in the direction of acceptance or triumph. One of the purposes of religious traditions being precisely to deal with the anxiety of death, one would hardly expect that the convinced religious consciousness would evince the same understanding of death as that held prior to the internalization of the transformative religious message.

Thus even the element of (relative) nonchalance in some strata of the Old Testament regarding death (or 'timely' death) should not automatically be construed as invalidation of the thesis that death is normatively experienced as existential threat. Rather, the heroic acceptance of death is made possible by internalization of the conviction that an individual's death finds its antidote in certain theological affirmations.

Bailey concedes this point when he addresses himself to the question as to how the ancient Israelites were able to cope (apparently) successfully with mortality. He mentions:

(1)   Their reliance on God's sovereign wisdom, care and power. Bailey cites Job: "The Lord gave, and the Lord has taken away; blessed be the name of the Lord." (Job 1:21) He then concludes: "Death therefore was not an irrational, intruding enemy but part of an ordered, controlled, harmonious creation." (Bailey 1979:57). But this confidence that God has a benevolent purpose even in our dying represents precisely a 'coping' strategy. It does not invalidate the interpretation that death is lamentable; it does assert, however, that there is a divine remedy for the plight of death.

(2) Bailey also points out that the conviction that human destiny is tied up with the larger group's fate rather than the individual's, plays a role in mitigating the threat of mortality. But this again is precisely the point: death would be intolerably threatening for many if it were not countered with the conviction that though they as individuals will perish, the group, the tribe, the nation, will prevail. It is this collective survival which bestows meaning and value, not the survival of discrete individuals.

(3) Bailey draws attention to the therapeutic value of recognizing that one's deeds and reputation will survive death in the memory of one's descendants.

"The memory of the righteous is a blessing, but the name of the wicked will rot." (Proverbs 10:7)

Moreover, says Bailey, "Even the persons without offspring could participate in the ongoing life of the community, through their influence, and be comforted." (Bailey 1979: 59, my italics)

The conclusion to be drawn is not the simple one that the ancient Israelite consciousness of death was serene and undistressed. Rather, it is that through their convictions about God, community and personal memory, they inhabited a cosmological realm in which the existential, i.e., universal anxiety of death was transformed into triumph over death.

It is only along the lines suggested by this distinction that one can hope to speak of a coherent Old Testament view or perspective on death.[2] Otherwise, one is left with contradictory evidence. Bailey disputes the traditional conception of the Old Testament's understanding of death but his more heroic and optimistic interpretation is contradicted by some of the texts he himself cites (eg., Ps. 22:14-15, Ps. 102:1-4, Isaiah 14:9-10). Conversely, an interpretation that sees only unrelieved despondency in the face of death fails to accommodate the textual evidence of the resolution of death-anxiety through faith in God and participation in his community.

Only by acknowledging that the Old Testament (like most religious traditions) contains both views, sometimes dialectically related, but more typically representing a 'raw' existential confrontation with finitude and mortality, on the one hand, and the internalization of a transformative message, on the other, can one accommodate the diverse scriptural testimonies.

2. Hebraic Holistic Anthropology

There are clear correlations between religious views of the self and conceptions of afterlife. Hinduism, for example, postulates the real self as transcendent and eternal spirit (<u>purusha</u> or <u>atman</u>) which correlates with the conceptions of afterlife that cluster around the term 'immortality of the soul'. Afterlife, in this context, is a spiritual eternity freed from the recalcitrant bondage of the flesh and psychic dispositions. While these ideas of self and immortality represent the highest view of human destiny, they are supplemented with the notion of a provisional stage in which the lower, phenomenal personality, under the sway of the law of karma, experiences a transient afterlife in a reincarnate form appropriate to the deeds of the previous life.

The biblical holistic view of the human as integrally composed of body and 'spirit' correlates with the view of afterlife expressed in the term 'resurrection of the body'. Additionally, the view of the human as a moral being with free will and responsibility implies the conviction that the afterlife involves a judgement according to the criterion of moral righteousness. Pursuant to this final judgement, the afterlife will be a condition of either blessing or punishment according to the moral quality of earthly deeds or, alternatively, the appropriation by faith of divine grace and forgiveness of sins. Of these two features of Hebraic anthropology -- the holistic and the moral -- the holistic perspective is perhaps the most determinative of Hebraic attitudes towards death and distinctive coping strategies, and to its elucidation we now turn.

An accurate assessment of ancient Israel's attitude towards biological death can be achieved only by first understanding the Hebraic view of man and his fate in the occurrence of death. Israelite anthropology is holistic. Dahl terms this, 'the unitive notion of human personality' (Dahl 1962: 59).

This is placed in the context of a wider category, 'the Semitic totality-concept'. A human being is a body animated by life-giving force or principle. This is conveyed in the Genesis myth of God forming man out of clay into which he then breathes his life-giving spirit (Hebrew: nephesh).

This story asserts or implies the following convictions:

(1) The significance of the bodily dimension of human existence. The formation of persons from clay means that the material, biological element is essential to human personality.

(2) God is the source of the life principle that animates and integrates the body, thus creating personhood. It is the divine breath that creates human life. The Hebrew terms nephesh or ruach signify breath which, in turn, signifies life-force; for breath is a sign of life.

The Yahwist version of the creation of man makes this clear: "The Lord God formed man of dust from the ground, and breathed into his nostrils the breath of life; and man became a living being." (Genesis 2:7)

Against this holistic anthropological background, death is viewed as the withdrawal, pouring out, or dissipation of the nephesh or vital principle. What remains is a shadowy, highly attenuated existence in Sheol -- the abode of the dead or 'shades'. (Hebrew: rephaim)

There is considerable difficulty in trying to conceptualize the status of the shades of Sheol. The survival of the shade is not the survival of an indestructible element such as the immortal soul in the Gita or Plato's Phaedo. In early, pre-apocalyptic, thought, the shade is not identified with the nephesh which has departed the body. Nor should the pouring out or loss of life-force be seen as the withdrawal to some transcendent realm of the enduring essential self, leaving only an accidental body-residue in Sheol. Such an interpretation would also falsely conflate early Hebraic thinking with that of Phaedo or the Gita. Rather, the loss of nephesh means the loss of essential personhood. The holistic anthropology demands the presence of both elements. Apart from body (-mind), or apart from the life-force, there is no significant selfhood. The shade in <u>Sheol</u> is "the person reduced to its weakest possible state" (Bailey 1979: 46).

In seeking to articulate this condition following death it might be said, in distinction to animistic, Indic, and Hellenistic anthropology in which it is the soul that survives death, that early Hebraic anthropology visualizes the survival of the body. This bodily reflection that survives the loss or pouring out of the life-force is clearly not, however, full bodily life, but a highly attenuated, weak residue. The life-force being effectively gone, earthly bodily energies and functions also vanish. But instead of contemplating a nihilistic extinction, the early Old Testament stratum believes in the survival of a shadowy, impoverished reflection of the bodily self which retains some reduced psychological functions. However, so diminished and disintegrated is the shade's bodily residue that survival in <u>Sheol</u> might be -- ambiguously -- spoken of as a disembodied existence.

The Hebraic holistic anthropology, however, needs further clarification. To describe it as holistic might convey the sense that no duality whatsoever is entertained in the Hebraic understanding of the person. But this is not so. A certain distinction is implied between a person's body and the life-principle (<u>nephesh</u>) that animates it, and whose loss means the effective disintegration of vital personality. However, because of the centrality of the life force in personality, the term '<u>nephesh</u>' can often signify the person. Thus when the prophet Ezekiel proclaims, "The soul (<u>nephesh</u>) that sins shall die" (Ezek. 18:4) this means that the person who breaks God's law shall be punished by death.[4]

It must be borne in mind that this type of Hebraic 'duality' cannot be assimilated to traditional Western (Greek-derived) dualisms of body and spirit, where spirit is understood as comprising mental qualities of reason, imagination, and affinity with the divine. A case, far-fetched though it seem, may be made that the Hebraic view of man resembles, in some respects, the dominant Upanishadic view in Hindu tradition. There, qualities of reason and consciousness are subsumed under the phenomenal self, which is transcended by the real self, the eternal spiritual <u>atman</u>. The congruity between Hebraic and Upanishadic views is restricted, however, to their conception of the 'bodily' self as comprising both physical and mental dimensions. They differ radically in their conception of the non-bodily element. For the Upanishads it is the immortal <u>atman</u>; for the Hebrews it is the divinely bestowed life-principle. One might say the Hebrew tradition remains resolutely biologicalist and eschews a metaphysical transformation of the vital principle.

This idea, alluded to above, of 'body' comprising also 'mind', may be further seen in the Hebraic conception of the shades (<u>rephaim</u>). What survives in <u>Sheol</u> seems to be neither body (narrowly construed as full physical entity), nor a disembodied mind. Rather, the shade is the body-mind element, <u>but deprived of its vitality</u>, and hence constituting only a highly reduced and weakened reflection of its earthly reality.

In the light of this understanding of death, the inference follows that survival in <u>Sheol</u> as a shade -- a weak and fragmentary reflection of one's full earthly life -- is not a source of consolation in the face of death, but, rather, of despair.

3. <u>Development of Hebraic Conceptions of Afterlife</u>

(a) <u>Survival in Sheol</u>

We may detect four different levels of survival of death in the Hebraic tradition. There is, first of all, the sort of bare survival sketched above, namely, a survival in <u>Sheol</u> which is inhabited by shades (<u>rephaim</u>) which are fragmentary, highly attenuated reflections of the human person after death. But, as we noted, it would be a serious mistake to understand this survival in <u>Sheol</u> as a kind of coping therapy because, in fact, survival in <u>Sheol</u> is part of the problem. We examined whether or not death is experienced as existential anxiety in the Old Testament or Hebrew scriptures and I concluded that in spite of certain contrary critics, the Hebraic tradition is consistent with other religious traditions in this respect. Death <u>is</u> viewed as an existential threat, as a threat to one's well-being, to one's survival, 'survalue' and esteem. It is experienced as a threat, in part, because the prospect of existence after death as a shade in <u>Sheol</u> is dreary and despondent. For survival of the shade is not, as we have noted, the survival of a positive, indestructible element such as the immortal soul. At this stage in Hebraic conceptual development, the surviving element is not to be identified with the nephesh or vital personality. It is not an indestructible soul; it is, rather, as Bailey says, the person reduced to its weakest possible state. So survival in Sheol or hades -- as a weakened and fragmented shadow of one's former self -- is not a reassurance in the face of death, but rather a source of dread. 'Those who go down to sheol do not praise God'. Their vital biological life has ceased; they are alienated from the community, and even estranged from the worship of God:

> For in death there is no remembrance of thee;
> in Sheol who can give thee praise? (Psalm 6;
> cf., Psalm 39:9 and 88:10)

Another passage depicting the despair of post-mortem existence as a shade in Sheol is Isaiah 14:9-11:

> Sheol beneath is stirred up
> to meet you when you come,
> it rouses the shades to greet you,
> all who were leaders of the earth;
> it raises from their thrones
> all who were kings of the nations.

> All of them will speak and say to you:
> "You too have become as weak as we!
> You have become like us!"

> Your pomp is brought down to Sheol,
> the sound of your harps;
> maggots are the bed beneath you,
> and worms are your covering.

(b) Collective Immortality

In the face of this prospect of biological extinction and shadowy survival in Sheol, a positive, therapeutic or coping answer is given. It is the answer of communal immortality. The fundamental human unit is found not in the individual but in corporate existence itself. Wheeler Robinson's famous phrase 'corporate personality' underscores the point that the human unit of existence is thought of not primarily in individual terms but in terms of the collectivity, in this case the nation, Israel. This offers some consolation in the face of death because one can experience the ongoing life of the community even in

the face of one's own demise. I, as an individual, may
go down to _Sheol_, but my people in whom I find my
identity continues.   So long as the collectivity
survives I shall survive in some sense.   Robert Jay
Lifton, the psychologist, in outlining various kinds of
immortality, lists first what he calls 'the biological
mode of immortality', but which I prefer to call
collective or communal immortality.   The biological
mode of immortality is described as:

> the sense of living on through, but in an
> emotional sense _with_ or even _in_ one's sons and
> daughters and their sons and daughters, by
> imagining an endless chain of biological
> attachment. This mode has found its classical
> expression in East Asian culture, especially
> in the traditional Chinese family system, but
> is of enormous importance in all cultures, and
> may well be the most universally significant
> of man's modes of immortality. Nor does it
> ever remain purely biological, but in varying
> degrees extends itself into social dimensions,
> into the sense of surviving through one's
> tribe, organization, people, nation or even
> species, that is, living on in any or all of
> these. (Lifton 1970: 22)

According to Milton Gatch (1969), death anxiety
among the ancient Israelites was handled by 1)
affirmation of the people's centrality in human
existence, and 2) by confidence in its survival.   To
affirm the people's centrality means that human
identity and value are understood in terms of the
group's reality, not in terms of individual
personality.

Soteriological survival (in contrast to dreary
survival in _Sheol_), in the framework of early Hebraic
thought, means survival of the people.   In this regard
we may note Abraham's death-bed concern for Isaac's
wife, which is really a preoccupation with the issue of
descendents. (Gen. 24: 1-9)   Abraham had neglected to
provide for the continuation of the line after Isaac --
a grave oversight given the indispensibility of the
collectivity's continuity if the anxiety of death is to
be assuaged.   It should be understood, however, that
immortality through the collectivity is more than
survival in the memory of descendents.   It is, as Gatch
says, an _organic_ conception.   The people itself is the
locus of human meaning and continuity.   As long as the

nation or people lives, so long will humans be essentially undying.

But certain limitations to this notion of collective immortality come quickly to the fore. First is the discernment that the collectivity itself may not be invulnerable to destruction. This is precisely the point Lifton is making in Boundaries from which I cited above. The emergence of nuclear weapons has threatened, perhaps destroyed, the consolation of those who found an antidote for the anxiety of death in their confidence in collective survival. The prospect of total annihilation of humanity with nuclear weapons now invalidates such confidence. It is now possible to conceive not only the extermination of one's nation, but that of the entire human species. On not so extreme a scale as that, ancient Israel also had to face the possibility of the people's historical destruction. Throughout her history Israel was buffeted by powerful pagan empires. The northern kingdom of Israel was vanquished by the Assyrians in 720 B.C., Judah fell to the Babylonians in 586 B.C. resulting in the captivity and fifty year exile of the national elite. The supervening military and political hegemony of Persia worked to ancient Israel's benefit, because it meant deliverance from captivity in Babylon and the return of the exiles. The domination of the Hellenistic Seleucids over Israel and their enforced program of deculturation is reflected in the Book of Daniel.

In the face of such historical calamity and domination of the covenant people by alien powers not similarly related to the Lord God of history, it was possible to simply apostatize. Yahweh is not more powerful than the Gods of Babylon or Assyria, of Persia or the Greeks. The contradiction of one's hopes by sobering historical reality may be resolved by abandoning the basic premise of God's sovereign, providential control over historical events. Some did, in fact, abandon the worship of Yahweh in just such a way.

In the normative scriptures of Israel, however, the contradiction between faith in God's historical rule and covenantal care by the actual historical events of conquest and subjugation, was handled by projecting God's triumph over wickedness and the final vindication of his people into the future. In other terms, Israel's ultimate resolution of the problems posed by evil, including death, was eschatological. Though the fortunes of the collectivity might look vulnerable in the face of present vicissitudes, nevertheless at some future point in God's good time, in the day of the Lord, he would intervene and restore the nation Israel.

In the early period, this was viewed, for the most part, as a literal historical restoration, normally conceived of as the restoration of the Davidic kingly line. This political and social rehabilitation of the Israelite collectivity which grounded confidence in the face of death, would take place in the future through God's historical intervention. The eschatological element thus introduced, provides the framework within which future Hebraic discussion about death and afterlife thereafter continued -- though in varying ways.

(c) Blessed Eternity for the Individual: Permanency of the Individual's Relation to God

A critical factor in the evolution of Hebraic ideas of afterlife is the emergence of conviction about the importance of the individual. It seems that for a long period of ancient Hebraic history the sense of collective personality, and confidence in the permanency of the larger social unit, was sufficient to legitimate hopes. But gradually the conviction emerged that the individual in his or her own right has an important status which has to be respected and somehow fulfilled. The emergence of the individual seen, perhaps, preeminently in the prophet Jeremiah contributed decisively to a mutation in ancient Israel's thought about afterlife.

We have seen that in an earlier period the idea of corporate personality had been strong enough to temper the anxiety of death and Sheol. And even when the collective vulnerability of Israel to historical calamity, conquest and exile became transparent, the initial therapeutic move consisted of the eschatological idea of national historical vindication. In Ezekiel's vision of the reconstitution of the dry bones, for example, the emphasis was still on corporate restoration. But now we find something different; we encounter a consciousness of individual concerns. In the face of this new perception of the importance of the individual, the old coping mechanism, the old therapeutic doctrine of the survival of the collectivity was now deemed inadequate because the question was asked: What about the fate of the individual upon death? Novel reflection was prompted by this consideration of the individual's destiny, not only in this life but also upon death, and led to transformation of Hebraic conceptions of afterlife.

There is a further factor, of the highest importance, that explains the mutation in ancient Israel's thought concerning death and afterstates. This is the recognition of God's character as gracious and sovereign love and, as a corollary to that, the permanency of the individual's relationship with God. In theological reflection upon the relation between God and the devotee, two convictions emerged. First, the relation of love and obedience between the devotee (I avoid the word 'believer' because it is too intellectualist a term) and God was so intense and valuable, that it was unthinkable that it should be terminated by biological death. Second, the very character of God as love and sovereign power precluded the defeat of his loving purpose towards persons by the intervention of death. The loving relationship initiated by the gracious covenant-making God and consummated by the devotees' response of faith could not be subject to the contingent circumstances of death.

Death is so arbitrary, so accidental; one can be in the fullness of life one moment, and dead the next. The point can be illumined by modern analogies. Can the loving relationship between the devotee and God be subject to someone having a drink too many before climbing into a car and precipitating a highway massacre? Can the relationship be terminated by taking a trip to a foreign country, ingesting some tiny micro-organism for which the individual has no immunity, getting sick and dying? Can capricious death annihilate the relation between God and persons?

The writers of the Hebrew scriptures eventually answered this question in the negative. God's loving purpose which brings into being the relationship of the devotee and God cannot be overcome by the accident of death. Accordingly, we note the emergence of a conception (not yet the developed idea of the resurrection of the body) of what we may call blessed afterlife. Some kind of survival of death in which the individual is not estranged from the blessed presence of God is assured. Intimations of this are found in

Psalm 16:9-1

> Thou dost not give me up to sheol,
> or let thy godly one see the Pit.
> Thou dost show me the path of life;
> in thy presence there is fullness of joy,
> in thy right hand are pleasure for evermore.

This evinces a growing conviction that the loving relationship with God is not sundered by death.

The same note is struck in Psalm 73:24,26

> Thou dost guide me with thy counsel,
> and afterward thou wilt receive me to glory;
> My flesh and my heart may fail,
> but God is the strength of my heart
> and my portion for evermore.[4]

As John Shaw, a Canadian scholar of an earlier generation said: The conviction of a blessed life after death "is essentially an argument from the nature and character of God; from the impossibility of God calling men into a fellowship with Himself here on earth, and then leaving them at last to perish in the dust." (Shaw 1945: 12-13)

(d) 'Soul' in Later Judaism

The growing confidence in God's love, justice, fidelity, and power led to the conviction (though unphilosophically developed) of life with God beyond the grave. It is in God's character to be the God of the living which, paradoxically, means that he is also the God of the dead whom he maintains in life in fulfillment of his promises to them.

In due course, this conviction about life in the presence of God beyond the grave, coalesced with the idea of a soul; that is, of an immortal dimension of the human personality that logically reinforced the certitude of blessed post-mortem life. In effect, the nephesh or life principle, became an immortal soul which would be the recipient of divine judgement after death to redress the imbalances of terrestrial justice. Sheol becomes the place of disembodied souls and is further divided into an abode for the good (Paradise) and one for the wicked (Gehenna). "The shades in She'ol are now souls or spirits ... A body/soul dualism has begun to function." (Silberman

1969: 30-1) This notion of a 'soul' was appropriated by some strands within the apocalyptic tradition and by the Pharisees. This provided a further dimension to the theological milieu in which the thinking of Jews and early Christians about death was subsequently forged.

(e) Resurrection of the Body

So far we have noted how the emergent idea of the role and value of the individual, and theological reflection upon the experience of loving relationship to God, called into question the previous understanding of Sheol as the fate of those who die -- a fate where there is no divine presence and communal link. Yet another factor hovers in the background; that is the demand of Israel's holistic anthropology. In the light of this Hebraic understanding of humans that stresses the importance of bodily existence in personality, it remained difficult, if not impossible, for Hebraic thought, as long as it remained rooted in its traditional antecedents, to conceptualize any kind of vital survival that did not entail a body. To be fully, vitally human means to have a body. Not, of course, a body which is a recalcitrant downward-dragging force imprisoning the self, and from which one needs to be liberated; but a body which is a divinely created good and an essential and valuable component of personal existence.

Normative Hebrew biblical anthropology should not be understood as a synthesis of psyche and soma as if each component had an independent existence prior to its fusion in the human being. The Gita and the Phaedo maintain that the soul exists prior to and independently of its temporary incarceration in the body. Much subsequent Christian thought would hold something similar -- at least an existence independent of the body following God's creation of the soul at a certain point in time. Hebraic anthropological unity is radical; body and life-force normally have no existence apart from the other. The departure of the vital principle means a disintegration of the body; conversely, the decomposition of the body entails the loss of life-force. A small exception noted by Aubrey Johnson, a Welsh scholar of the Old Testament, is the possible existence of the life-force in a highly weakened form, in association with scattered bodily remains like bones. Apart from that, bodily disintegration signals the departure of the vital force. The human, in Hebraic terms, should be more accurately thought of as a body-life, or body-power unity, rather than a body-mind or body-spirt unity which can give the misleading impression of a self-subsisting soul entity that can be and has been drawn from these conventional terms of psyche and soma, soul and body.

The inference to be drawn from this holistic anthropology is that if there are any grounds for affirming a blessed life after death for individuals -- such as the love and power of God transcending the contingency of death -- then this must ultimately take the form of a bodily resurrection. Even after the notion of nephesh was transmuted into that of an independently existing soul that survives death, the conviction prevailed that resurrection of the body is required for full everlasting life. Pre-existent Hebraic attitudes, such as the crucial, holistic conception of humans, afforded an hospitable theological matrix for the assimilation or generation of eschatological ideas of the resurrection of the body.

With the emergence of apocalyptic, the doctrine of resurrection of the body comes to the fore. Apocalyptic is a perspective that sees the present world order as debased and doomed and places in opposition to it a trans-mundane order that will become actual following a dramatic divine intervention. Iranian cosmic or metaphysical dualism becomes fused with Hebraic ethical and temporal dualism. The Book of Daniel, composed during the Maccabean period (c. 168 B.C.) in response to the persecution perpetrated by the hellenizing Seleucid, Antiochus Epiphanes, reflects the apocalyptic influence and the doctrine of resurrection of the body: "And many of those who sleep in the dust of the earth shall awake, some to everlasting life, some to shame and everlasting contempt". (Daniel 12:2)

An earlier reference in which an allusion to resurrection of the body has frequently been seen is from the prophet Isaiah:

The dead shall live, their bodies shall arise.
O dwellers in the dust, awake and sing for joy! (Isaiah 26:19)

Some critics have opined that the early date (8th

cent. B.C.) indicates a metaphorical reference to the nation's restoration. At face value, however, the passage does seem to point to a literal statement of the bodily resurrection of individual devotees of Yahweh. If an holistic anthropology is a presupposition of Israelite consciousness, there is no reason why this conviction of bodily resurrection should not emerge spontaneously in prophetic faith. An alternative interpretation is that this Isaianic reference to bodily resurrection represents a later interpolation.[5]

The idea of bodily resurrection that came to the fore during the intertestamental period was by no means uniform. In some cases it envisioned a resurrection of all followed by a final judgement; in other instances only the righteous would be raised. The common note that was sounded was hope and gratitude for God's final triumph over evil and death.

NOTES

1. Bailey does not claim to be innovating "this much rarer approach". He explicitly associates his views with those of Walter Brueggemann: "A substantial challenge to the ubiquitous claim that the fear of death is universal (and is of such severity that it is repressed) is presented by Walter Bruggemann's assessment: within the biblical historical context and faith-understanding, death was 'not particularly feared'." (Bailey 1979: 4)

2. It is true that Bailey alludes to a "range of reflection" upon death within the Old Testament. But there is little doubt which dimension is regarded as predominant and normative: It is that which affirms "death as a natural event" with the result that "the Yahwists of ancient Israel seem to have been less anxious about mortality than were their neighbours". (Bailey 1979: 101)

3. My criticism of Bailey is echoed by John Munroe in his review of Biblical Perspectives on Death: "Bailey appears to over-react to the Pauline view [of death as enemy]." Scottish Journal of Theology, Vol. 34 No. 1.

4. In confirmation, cf., "On the O.T. view, man has no soul, but the Hebrew term (nephesh) translated 'soul' in the modern versions denotes a psycho-physical totality, corresponding to that which we mean when we talk of a living being and its different modes of expression." (Article 'Man' in J.J. Von Allmen, ed., A Companion to the Bible New York: Oxford, 1958.)

5. Some commentators have also seen a reference to blessed immortality in Job 19:27-7

> For I know that my Redeemer lives,
> and at last he will stand upon the earth;
>
> and after my skin has been thus destroyed;
> then without my flesh, I shall see God.

REFERENCES

Bailey, Lloyd
    1979   Biblical Perspectives on Death. Philadelphia: Fortress Press.

Dahl, M.E.
    1962 The Resurrection of the Body. London: SCM.

Gatch, Milton C.
    1969 Death: Meaning and Morality in Christian Thought and Contemporary Culture. Seabury Press. Reprinted in part in Edwin S. Schneidman, Death: Current Perspectives (Palo Alto, California: Mayfield Publishing, 1976).

Lifton, Robert Jay
    1970 Boundaries: Psychological Man in Revolution. New York: Vintage Books.

Shaw, John Mackintosh
    1945 Life After Death: The Christian View of the Future Life. Toronto: Ryerson Press.

Silberman, Lou H.
    1969 "Death in the Hebrew Bible and Apocalyptic Literature" in Liston O. Mills, ed., Perspectives on Death. Nashville: Abingdon Press.

CHAPTER SIX

RESURRECTION OF THE BODY IN CHRISTIAN TRADITION

1. Resurrection of the Body in the Gospels

Intertestamental apocalyptic exercises a profound impact on Jesus and the early church in the formation of their thinking about death and afterlife. Jesus draws upon the apocalyptic current in the atmosphere of his time.[1] A case in point is the passage in the Gospel of Mark chapter twelve, about levirate marriage. Jesus' ill-intentioned interrogators are Sadducees, members of the priestly and patrician party of Jewish society of this time. The Sadducees who viewed only the Pentateuch as revealed scripture, denied the resurrection.

> And Sadducees came to him, who say there is no resurrection; and they asked him a question, saying, "Teacher, Moses wrote for us that if a man's brother dies and leaves a wife, but leaves no child, the man must take the wife, and raise up children for his brother. There were seven brothers; the first took a wife, and when he died left no children; and the second took her, and died, leaving no children; and the third likewise; and the seven left no children. Last of all the woman also died. In the resurrection whose wife will she be? For the seven had her as wife. (Mark 12: 18-27).

The Sadducees are trying to attack both Jesus and the Pharisaic doctrine of resurrection by reducing it to absurdity. They do so by drawing upon the Mosaic injunction of levirate marriage, that is to say, the religious requirement that if a man dies and leaves no children, his brother has an obligation to marry the deceased brother's wife and generate children in order to continue the family line.

Levirate marriage may be clarified by noting the Old Testament passage in which Onan comes under divine judgement for spilling his seed on the ground. Many an adolescent has been harried by the warning that Onan's fate will be his fate if the adolescent engages in masturbation, for this text has provided the biblical sanction against it. But most scholars are of the opinion that what comes under condemnation is not masturbation but, rather, failure to observe the injunction of levirate marriage. Onan's religious, moral obligation was not to enjoy his deceased brother's wife without any commensurate responsibilities. His duty was to raise up progeny for his brother, and by spilling his seed upon the ground he violated this religious legal requirement.

The institution of levirate marriage is the context of this confrontation between Jesus and the Sadducees. Their game plan is that by showing the ridiculousness of seven brothers having to compete for the one wife when they all enter the resurrection age, they will have invalidated the whole notion of the resurrection of the body.

> Jesus said to them, "Is not this why you are wrong, that you know neither the scriptures nor the power of God? For when they rise from the dead, they neither marry nor are given in marriage, but are like angels in heaven. And as for the dead being raised, have you not read in the book of Moses, in the passage about the bush, how God said to him, 'I am the God of Abraham, and the God of Isaac, and the God of Jacob?' He is not the God of the dead, but of the living, you are quite wrong." (Mark 12: 24, 27).

We have two points here. First of all Jesus puts himself solidly on the side of the apocalyptic belief in the resurrection of the body, the notion that God is the God of the living and that, therefore, the afterlife cannot permanently and ultimately be a place of non-vital shadowy existence like <u>Sheol</u>. Belief in such a post-mortem destiny in <u>Sheol</u> would invalidate the theological conviction that God is the God of those who are truly and fully alive, and not the God of marginally live shadows. A second point is that life in the resurrection age transcends our normal human understandings. It is not the case that because there was the marriage of seven brothers to a single woman in this life that in the resurrection age they would be confronted with the problem of choice. In heaven they neither give nor are given in marriage. The resurrection condition transcends our normal human understandings of how social relations work.

This teaching of Jesus about the afterlife is given almost incidentally in the context of the debate between Pharisees and Saducees about the possibility of genuine life after death. Though Jesus shows himself an advocate of the notion of resurrection of the body, the burden of Jesus' message is not an answer to the question "What happens to me when I die?" His main message is the nearness of God's kingdom and the need for repentance, the need for faith. At the beginning of his public career, Jesus came into Nazareth preaching that the kingdom of God is at hand, that is, that the rule of God was not only imminent, but had, in fact, already begun in his words and deeds. In the face of this divine intervention in history for humanity's redemption, the only appropriate response was to repent, to turn away from one's old life and to have faith in this good news of God's gracious action on mankind's behalf. This message of cosmic salvation is Jesus' chief concern.

Death is pertinent, however, in that human mortality exacerbates the experience of human insecurity and heightens the sense of urgency respecting human response. In effect, the hearers are warned, "Make your response now while you still have the opportunity to do so." Thus, though Jesus is not concerned primarily to proclaim a salvific message that answers the question about what happens after death, death remains important as the horizon against which a decision of faith must be made. He assumes that after death there will be a bodily resurrection.

The Christian tradition subsequent to Jesus shares the apocalyptic views of the Pharisees appropriated by Jesus, but to Jesus' perceptions they add one significant ingredient, namely, their conviction that Jesus has been raised from the dead. One of the elements of the apocalyptic understanding of the end point when God's kingdom comes, is that there will be resurrection. Because Jesus was raised from the dead, the earliest strand of Christianity affirms the conviction that the end days have already begun. The eschatological consummation is already unfolding, the proof being that Jesus has been raised from the dead. Their religious, cultural heritage asserted that when the resurrection of the dead occurred they would be in the end time; Jesus was resurrected; therefore, the end times must have dawned.

That is one way of putting the argument. There is another possibility that I shall simply suggest. The argument may be reversed. These earliest Christians had experienced some of the gifts that were to be made available only in the end times, gifts like the presence of God, forgiveness of sins, the spirit's ethical power to renew life and transform it in the direction of love. Because they had experienced reconciliation with God and the other spiritual gifts associated with the apocalyptic consummation, they would have assumed the existence of the other sign of the end, namely, resurrection. It could be argued that Jesus' resurrection was a necessary logical corrollary for people who believed that the divine intervention at the end of days had occurred because they had experienced the gifts that attend it.[2] The more orthodox interpretation, of course, maintains that the primitive community, because it was convinced of the fact of Jesus' resurrection, moved to the inference that the new age, the time of God's kingdom, had dawned.

2. The Teaching of Paul on the Resurrection

With Paul we are at a decisive point in Christian teaching about death and afterlife because his first letter to the Corinthians is the locus classicus of Christian discussion about resurrection of the body. It is necessary to bear in mind that ideas are not self generating and free floating, but have a connection with the social and cultural conditions of the thinkers who hold them. Paul's formulation of his doctrine of resurrection takes place in encounter with contrary and conflicting opinions. Mystery cults, Orphism, Eleusinian mysteries, but principally Gnostic movements were part of his social and intellectual milieu. Gnosticism is a complex phenomenon, but to put the matter simply, it is a movement which has internalized a conflict dualism. By this is meant the notion that there are in human existence two metaphysical forces locked in irreconcilable conflict. There is the force of light, spirit, and goodness; opposed to it, there is a force of darkness, matter, and wickedness. Humans are caught in this arena of conflicting forces and their well-being requires that they find deliverance from the power of darkness and evil. The means of emancipation is gnosis, secret knowledge, which is delivered by those who stand in a line of transmission from some primitive oracle.

Salvation usually, though not necessarily, entails the mediation of a divine being whose teachings make possible emancipation from material bondage.

We are close here to the metaphysical atmosphere exuded by the Gita of the Hindu tradition. We noted there a conflict dualism, a clear differentiation between spirit and matter. The essential human reality, the true and good self, is spirit. Unfortunately, spirit has become entangled with materiality, with bodily existence, necessitating release from this bodily incarceration.

One can imagine the Gnostic reaction to the doctrine of resurrection of the body. We get some intimation of this when Paul preached his sermon on the Aereopagus, or Mars Hill, in Athens (Acts 17: 22-34). Though not necessarily Gnostics, his Greek audience would have been, at the very least,familiar with this conflict dualism differentiating spirit which is true, real and good, on the one hand, from matter which is ultimately evil and damaging to the spirit, on the other, and from which the spirit needs to be liberated. In this milieu Paul preached the idea of bodily resurrection, and was greeted with a ridiculing response. They told him that they would hear further about this on another occasion, but, in truth, they thought it was amusing. Here was a man telling them that human fulfillment entailed resurrection of the body. To this their logical response to Paul might well have been "Fool! Our problem is to be delivered from the body! Having been delivered from this present one at the point of death, the last thing we want is another, because it is bodily existence which is the source of the spirit's bondage and human degradation."

It was in that Hellenistic, Gnostic environment, which visualizes the spirit as the essential component of personality and the body as a damaging prison house of the soul, that Paul had to forge his understanding of resurrection of the body. His first letter to the Corinthians, chapter 15, is an elucidation of the Christian teaching or resurrection written with one eye on the community of believers, and the other on the Gnostic competitors who sought to communicate a different redemptive goal that would not involve resurrection of the body. It begins with Paul reminding his readers of Christ's resurrection by reciting a tradition which he has received. He says, in effect, "I remind you that when I talk about the resurrection of Christ, I am transmitting only what I myself first received; I did not make it up. This tradition declares that Christ died for our sins in accordance with the scriptures, that he was buried, and that he was raised on the third day in accordance with the scriptures." This capsule statement of the tradition constitutes a primitive Christian catechism. The primitive kerygma -- the primitive declaration of faith -- was that Christ died for human sins in accordance with the scriptures, which means that Jesus' atoning death on the cross is viewed as the fulfillment of Old Testament prophecy. His being raised on the third day is also in accordance with Hebrew scriptural prophecy. Then he appeared to Cephas or Peter, subsequently to the twelve, and then to more than five hundred at one time, most of whom were still alive as Paul wrote, though some had fallen asleep, that is, had died. The inference seems to be that Paul was exhorting his readers to check with those who were eye witnesses of the risen Lord if they did not believe him. The risen Christ later appeared to James, then to all the apostles, and last of all, as to one untimely born, he appeared also to Paul. Paul considered his meeting with Jesus on the Damascus road to have been, not a subjective vision, but a real encounter with the resurrected Christ.

Paul goes on to say that if Christ is preached as raised from the dead, how can some say there is no resurrection of the dead? But who could be asserting that there is no resurrection of the dead? The dissidents are probably Gnostics or more likely Gnostic Christians. Even if Gnostics existed as an independent religious body, it is probable that Paul is here addressing Gnostics who have integrated themselves with the emerging church to create a syncretistic Christianity.

Paul then continues his doctrinal exposition by stating that if there is no resurrection of the dead, then Christ has not been raised. This represents an interesting inversion of argument. He might have been expected to say that if Christ is not raised, then there is no resurrection of the dead. But what he does say is that if, in principle, there is no resurrection of the dead, then Christ could not have been raised. But, in fact, Christ has been raised from the dead, the first fruits of those who have fallen asleep. To get the significance of this requires that we keep the apocalyptic context in mind. One of the things that is supposed to happen at the end-time when God intervenes in history to vanquish wickedness and to inaugurate his kingdom of righteousness, is the resurrection of the dead. Jesus' resurrection is not an idiosyncratic event; it signals the beginning of the general resurrection that occurs in the end times. That the end of history has been initiated is disclosed by the resurrection of Jesus.

Paul's argument then assumes an intriguing social or collective direction. "For as by a man came death, by a man has come also the resurrection of the dead. For as in Adam all die, so also in Christ shall all be made alive." (I Corinthians 15: 21-22) These verses convey a complex view about collective identity. We noted earlier the idea of corporate personality in the Hebrew scriptures; this survives into the New Testament period. Because the first human, Adam, sinned and, in consequence, died, the whole human race deriving from Adam also sins and dies. Humanity does not exist as an assembly of discrete individuals each one forging his own destiny but, rather, as a corporate body that inherits Adam's condition. Paul is bound to the Genesis tradition that death is a consequence of sin; if Adam had not introduced an imbalance into the world by his defiance of God, if Adam had not aspired to be like God, then he and his human descendants would have been immortal. Mortality is a consequence of sin. (Romans 5: 12). As Paul says, "The wages of sin is death." (Romans 6: 23) Because Adam sinned the whole human collectivity is subject to sin and death.

A new person, however, has been inserted into history; a second Adam has appeared in the person of Jesus Christ. According to Paul, mankind is being reconstituted by God. Now there is a new humanity deriving from the new Adam -- Christ. To place one's trust in Christ is to move out of the collectivity of the first Adam -- the body of sin and death -- into the new collectivity of the second Adam -- the body of Christ. Because Christ has been raised from the dead, all those who are in the collectivity of the new Adam will share his resurrection, just as previously they suffered the legacy of the first Adam's sin and mortality.[3]

"But each in its own order." Resurrection happens in a sequence: "Christ, the first fruits; then, at his [second] coming those who belong to Christ. Then comes the end, when he delivers the kingdom to God the Father after destroying every rule and every authority and power." (I Corinthians 15: 23-24)   One senses the powerful apocalyptic atmosphere in which this is written.   The action of Christ is presented as a continuing struggle against all the ungodly forces that conspire against God's perfect rule and mankind's eternal felicity.   "Christ must reign until he has put all his enemies under his feet.   The last enemy to be destroyed is death." (I Corinthians 15: 25-26)   This is one of the clearest statements that death is not a friend, death is not a 'natural' occurrence.   Even though death is inevitable and universal, it is still experienced as an absurd limit that contradicts the highest human aspirations.

Paul, we have seen, writes with his Gnostic adversaries in mind.   Against them, he insists that there is a resurrection of the body.   Paul operates with an holistic anthropology which cannot conceive of authentic human survival unless it entails bodily existence.   But Paul fights on two fronts.   Over against the literalists who think that it is the earthly physical body that is raised -- this material body which is subject to coronary infarct, cancer and muscular dystrophy -- he insists that the resurrection body cannot be this mundane body.   It must be a transformed body, a body adapted to the peculiar existence of a supernatural afterlife.   Accordingly, the doctrine of the resurrection of the body must not be interpreted in literal terms, although, admittedly, some Christians, Jews and Muslims do.

There is a large painting in the Tate Gallery in London which depicts the resurrection of the body at the end of historical time.   The stone slabs have been lifted off the tombs and their occupants are shown waking, sitting up and coming out of the tombs.   That is the materialistic way some visualize the resurrection of the body; it is very literal minded.   A number of ancient Jewish and Muslim graves are localized in the Kidron Valley outside Jerusalem because of the belief that the resurrection in the last days will begin at Jerusalem; consequently people had themselves buried there in order to be first on hand when the last trumpet sounded!   There are rabbinical stories of subterranean migration of bodies, so that if someone was buried in Cracow they would travel through the earth in order to be in the Holy Land, in Zion, when the resurrection occurred.

Paul, in contrast, shares with some of the rabbinic thinkers of his time, a type of transcendentalist notion of the resurrection state. It is not material; it is a transformed existence. Paul at this point is close to Jesus' thought when he says in heaven they neither give nor are given in marriage. The heavenly afterlife is a transformed existence in which social limitations of mundane life no longer apply. In sum, flesh and blood cannot inherit the Kingdom of Heaven.

But though the resurrection body is not the physical body, there still has to be a body because the holistic anthropology, as well as other factors which we shall examine shortly, demand it. So it is sown a perishable body but it is raised imperishable, or, as Paul says, alternatively, 'there is a physical body and there is also a spiritual body" (I Corinthians 15: 44). I think we must concede at this point that Paul is stumbling upon himself in an almost contradictory manner in trying to express, in halting and limited human language, his vision of these transcendent apocalyptic possibilities. A spiritual body is a body so empowered by the divine spirit that it is suitable for the transformed conditions of God's new age, of God's Kingdom. Paul declares this conviction about bodily transformation thus:

> Lo! I tell you a mystery. We shall not all sleep, but we shall all be changed, in a moment, in a twinkling of an eye, at the last trumpet. For the trumpet will sound, and the dead will be raised imperishable, and we shall be changed ... When the perishable puts on the imperishable, and the mortal puts on immortality, then shall come to pass the saying that is written:
>
> "Death is swallowed up in victory."
> "O death, where is thy victory?
> "O death, where is thy sting?"
>
> The sting of death is sin, and the power of sin is the law. But thanks be to God, who gives us the victory through our Lord Jesus Christ. (1 Cor.15: 51-57)

We may find hints of what Paul means by the "spiritual body" in the Gospel accounts of Jesus' resurrection body, e.g., it passes through locked doors eats fish and honeycomb, appears and disappears in widely separated places. There was continuity between Jesus' new body and his earthly body, but not identity. The two disciples bound for Emmaus, for instance, did not immediately recognize him when they met him as a stranger on the road. It was only later at the breaking of bread at mealtime that they became aware that their strange companion was the risen Lord.

The antecedents of the resurrection of the body go back, we discovered, several hundred years, but the doctrine receives a particular confirmation for Christians in that they hold that the resurrection of the last days has already begun in the resurrection of Jesus Christ. The belief in the resurrection of the dead was not grounded in the resurrection of Jesus Christ; in fact, it is the other way around. It is possible for Jesus Christ to be raised because it is in God's economy that the dead shall be raised. But now it has happened. The resurrection is no longer for Christians simply a matter of eschatological hope. It is a process that has begun in the resurrection of Jesus.

3. Difficulties

The new age of resurrection life has been objectively inaugurated by the resurrection of Christ, but it is subjectively appropriated by the individual disciple by faith in Christ. A new life in the Spirit -- also called eternal life by the evangelist John -- is thus begun within history but awaits resurrection for its fulfillment. The question emerges: When does the Christian's resurrection of the body take place? Immediately upon death? Only at the Last Day?

Influenced by a corporate sense of salvation -- a legacy of ancient Israel's experience of peoplehood and corporate personality -- the early church's main tendency was to view the resurrection as an event at the end of history when its climax is reached at the second coming of Christ.

But certain psychological uneasiness with this answer can be immediately perceived. What is the condition of those who have died in the Lord? What kind of existence do they enjoy prior to the second advent of the Lord and the consummation of history?

Are they merely in some sort of intermediate limbo? It is questions like these which have led some to conclude that judgement and resurrection take place immediately upon death and that, consequently, the bereaved can be consoled with the assurance that their beloved dead instantly and fully receive the blessings of heavenly life in the presence of God.

The difficulty with this, from the perspective of Christian faith, is that it seems to run counter to the biblical evidence on the subject. There it is held that those who die with faith in God and his grace undergo a waiting period in an intermediate state until the second coming of Christ and the final resurrection and judgement.

Not that they are absent from God and his care. They are said to be "in Abraham's bosom", to be "asleep in the Lord"; they are "with Christ", they are in paradise. Nevertheless, they do not yet enjoy the plenitude of heavenly life, and cannot, until their bodies are resurrected.

It is reluctance to acquiesce in this intermediate state of waiting or sleep that probably shifted Christian thought from robust belief in resurrection of the body, to a complex amalgam in which immortality of the soul predominates over resurrection as the primary therapy for the anxiety of death.

Associated with the teaching of the resurrection of the body is the idea of last judgement. The picture generally presented is that of a grand assize in which the living and the resurrected will pass before Christ to have their deeds and their spiritual status assessed. Those who are approved are assured of blessed eternal life in Heaven; those in whom sin prevails are consigned to eternal punishment in Hell.

For Christians particularly, this idea of judgement and retribution raises difficulties of compatability with the central Christian doctrine of justification by grace. There are various attempts to reconcile grace and recompense but we cannot go into them here.

4. An Existential Hermeneutic of the Resurrection of the Body

I want to indicate now what the doctrine of

resurrection of the body might mean to those who have internalized this message. Christians who recite the apostles' creed Sunday by Sunday, say as part of their fundamental declaration of theological conviction that they believe in the resurrection of the body. What are they affirming when they say, "I believe in the resurrection of the body"?

With the symbol of 'resurrection of the body' the Christian (and the Muslim and the Jewish) tradition affirms that the enemy death does not have the last word, but is vanquished by God's life-giving power. <u>Resurrection</u> is compressed information about a triumphant way of handling human anxiety of death.

(1) The resurrection symbol affirms a devotee's confidence in the loving care and power of God that suffices against all threats to human well-being including death. God's character is such that both his love and power preclude the finality of death's pain and irrationality.

(2) It conveys the conviction that the fellowship with God already enjoyed in this earthly life will not be terminated by death, but will flourish in life beyond. The Johannine teaching of eternal life as a present possession of those with faith in Christ which is perfected in the future consummation, is an eloquent statement of this view of continuity. (e.g., "He who believes in the Son has eternal life ..." John 3:36)

(3) By resurrection the devotee attests that the goodness that comes to him is the result of God's grace. Specifically, eternal life is not a consequence of an inherent human property, but is an act of God in which he gives to persons what by nature they do not possess -- immortality.

If humans by nature have, for example, an immortal soul, they will survive death regardless of divine love or intervention. The idea of resurrection of the body asserts that the afterlife is not a natural or inherent human destiny but, rather, an effect of divine love and grace. It is something that is given to the faithful, not something they possess as an intrinsic human property.

But these personal meanings could be adequately conveyed by the term 'resurrection' construed as a metaphor for God's gracious restorative activity towards his human creation which is under the threat of death. But the entire symbol consists of resurrection of the body. What further meanings about life, death, and afterlife, are intended by the addition of 'the body'?

Resurrection of the body is a way of affirming a particular analysis of human existence and prospects. Persons who say, "I believe in the resurrection of the body" are committing themselves to the conviction that:

(1)   The human enemy is sin, not the body. The body is not a prison house that temporarily confines and degrades the pure soul, and which must be escaped if the soul is to attain its highest plane. Were this the case, death would be welcomed as a friend, as the soul's liberator, and not as an enemy. The source of human evil is sin, by which is meant willful rebellion against God and estrangement from him. In this perspective, which goes back to the book of Genesis, death is the consequence of sin.

More strongly, in affirming the resurrection of the body, a disciple expresses commitment to the sanctity of the body. The body is not a recalcitrant and provisional liability; it is not intrinsically wicked. Rather, the body reflects the Creator's goodness and is a temple of his holy spirit (1 Cor. 6:19). Bodies even have a place in the transformed life of heaven.

(2)   The resurrection of the body bears witness that the total personality survives death. In contrast to survival as a de-vitalized, highly attenuated shade in Sheol; and in contrast, further, to Hellenistic ideas of survival of a disembodied, self-subsisting, immortal soul, the doctrine of resurrection of the body affirms the survival of the whole person. This is entirely consonant with the holistic

or unitive Hebraic anthropology that finds full personhood inconceivable apart from bodily existence.

(3)   Resurrection of the body declares that life after death entails identity and recognition. It will be the same person -- albeit transformed and perfected -- who is resurrected as was laid in the grave. The historical development of unique personality is not accidental but intrinsic to God's ultimate goal of human reclamation. This continuity of personal identity from earthly to post-resurrection state means that persons will recognize one another, and that affections and relations begun on earth will in some way endure into the transcendent kingdom of God. Obviously, this continuity has also a certain radical disjunction from earthly life because of the transformation dictated by other-worldly existence. Nevertheless what survives death is a particular and recognizable person and not an anonymous residue, partly because of the continuity of that person's bodily qualities and style.

This insight is conveyed by the story of Jesus' resurrection appearances. After Jesus' resurrection, the Gospel accounts tell us, his disciples recognized him -- albeit with some difficulty. It is the same Christ who was laid in Joseph of Arimathea's tomb, but not entirely the same, for he now lived with a transcendent and mysterious resurrection body, not mundane flesh and blood. It could materialize quickly, it seems, in various geographical locations. It was able to appear in Galilee, then in Judea. But though a transformed resurrection body, it was still a body that allowed the disciples, after some initial difficulties, to recognize the Lord. Two of the disciples walked with Jesus along the Emmaus Road on Easter Eve and conversed with him, but did not immediately know who he was. It was only after perceiving the peculiar gestures of the stranger as he shared supper with them, and as he broke and blessed the bread, that they recognized the Lord. Jesus was not dead after all; he had been raised! Bodily existence, though transformed, is the substratum of personal identity which permits recognition of persons in the afterlife.

Jesus resurrection is treated as a paradigm of the disciples' -- "We shall be like him" (1 John 3 2). Just as the risen Christ was recognized even so will the disciples be known to one another after the resurrection.

Since it is, in part, bodily characteristics that manifest unique identity and enable us to recognize one another in our ordinary existence, resurrection of the body is a way of claiming these same qualities for the resurrection afterlife.

(4)   To affirm the resurrection of the body is to affirm the cosmic sovereignty of God. All existence is within the scope of God's kingly rule. God is the king of the universe, not just the ruler of disembodied spirits. This means that God rules over the totality of the cosmos, including bodily, material existence because it is his creation.

(5)   Moreover, to hold that the body is resurrected is to hold that all creation is redeemable. God's comprehensive sovereignty aims at a gracious, redemptive goal even for nature, epitomized by the body.

Death is viewed both in Genesis and Corinthians as a consequence of sin. The radical egocentricity of humans disrupts the entire cosmic harmony. Even nature is vitiated by human sin, by rebellion against the Creator and rightful Ruler of the cosmos. Paul states "The whole creation has been groaning in travail together until now." (Romans 8:22) Specifically, "The sting of death is sin." (1 Cor. 15:56). The resurrection of the body signals the reversal of this process. Just as sin brought death, even so redemption from sin brings resurrection of the body.

All these various meanings are implicit in the doctrine of the resurrection of the body. There is a tendency to dismiss this doctrine prematurely as a rather curious and naive notion. An understanding of these inner or existential meanings of this doctrine, which I have briefly outlined, suggests that this teaching about the afterlife is more compelling than might at first glance seem.

NOTES

1. A provocative reversal of this interpretation of Jesus' perspective on the historical process is advanced by Cott. He says that earliest Christianity was anti-apocalyptic; it rejected facile convictions about the divine triumph over sadness, sin and death. Apocalypticism, according to Cott, falsifies the original New Testament teaching by substituting the triumph over death in the eschatological advent of the Son of Man for the primal kerygma which recognized life's existential finitude and limitation epitomized by death. The affirmation that the Messiah dies conveys the starkly life-confronting nature of the original message. In the place of this original message of inescapable human finitude and ambivalence, apocalyptic proffers an optimistic eschatological resolution of duality. The proclamation of a Messiah who died functions precisely to disabuse its hearers of an unwarranted optimism.

    This is true as far as it goes, but the New Testament message, I believe, is falsifed if the answering note of apocalyptic victory is not also sounded. Still, it is useful to remember that one is not permitted to rush too quickly towards eschatological resolutions of human pain and perplexity. The proclamation of the Messiah who died is a useful reminder that for humans -- as for the Messiah -- there is no crown without a cross.

2. I have argued in this way in my article, "The Resurrection: An Existential Verification" in The Christian Century, April 10, 1968. A more demythologized interpretation of the resurrection of Jesus is subsequently formulated in "The Resurrection as God's Historical Deed" in The Christian Century. April 7, 1971.

3. A cogent analysis of the Pauline understanding of human history as a conflictual interaction between the Adamic collectivity of sin and death, and the new collectivity of Christ is set out in John A.T Robinson, The Body: A Study in Pauline Theology (London: SCM).

REFERENCES

Cott, Jeremy
    1979   "The Problem of Christian Messianism".
    Journal of Ecumenical Studies. Vol. 16, No. 3,
    Summer.

CHAPTER SEVEN

NIRVANA AND THE UNREALITY OF THE SELF IN BUDDHISM

1. The Sway of Death

Our exploration of the interpretations of death and afterlife in some religious traditions moves now to a consideration of the Buddhist tradition. What analysis of the meaning of death and what coping mechanism in the face of death is proffered by Buddhists?

At the beginning of our investigation we rapidly surveyed some religious images that provided initial support for my assumptions that death is universally experienced as human threat, as pain, as problem, as enemy, to which the religious traditions seek to give a therapeutic answer, some kind of transformative solution. Now we shall examine the Buddhist tradition in more detail to see if the thesis that death is universally confronted with dread is validated.

It is necessary, to begin, to bring to mind once again the famous Buddhist four sights: sickness, death, old age and finally the bikshu, the monk or ascetic who inspires in Siddartha Guatama the possibility of redemption from the preceding three baleful conditions of life which had come to his attention. Already at the beginning of his career as a spiritual explorer there is an inchoate insight into the painful nature of life and an understanding of death as something which threatens human well-being. It subsequently became the Buddha's purpose to enunciate a spiritual message that would overcome this human suffering.

(a) The Four Noble Truths

When one refers to Buddhist religious truth, one immediately thinks, I imagine, of the Four Noble Truths. After his enlightenment at the age of thirty-five Siddartha Gautama, now the Buddha, the awakened one, arose from the tree of enlightenment under which he had been meditating and went off to the Deer Park near Varanasi (Banares) where he set in motion the wheel of the Dharma as the Buddhist teaching is called. He preached his first sermon to five ascetics with whom he had been associated earlier, and whom he had abandoned in order to devote himself to meditation and the attainment of enlightenment. This first sermon contains the Four Noble Truths. The first is that life is suffering. In spite of all appearances to the contrary and all temptations to think that life has some enduring happiness, the truth is that life is fundamentally at its core a vale of tears: life is suffering. The second noble truth is that the cause of suffering is thirst, that is, desire or craving: we suffer because we desire things. The third noble truth declares the possibility of the cessation of desire. With the cessation of desire the abolition of suffering follows. The fourth truth concerns the eight-fold path that leads to the cessation of desire and consequently the overcoming of suffering. These four noble truths -- the first one specifically -- dramatically present the Buddha's insight that life is intrinsically suffering. A key indicator of the character of life as suffering is the presence of death; suffering is signalled primarily by death.

This analysis of human existence is echoed in the Buddha's final words at the age of eighty after forty-five years preaching the four noble truths which established the reign of Dharma, of truth. After his final meal of what is assumed to have been poisoned mushrooms, he said, "Compounded things decay -- strive earnestly." The Buddhist analysis asserts that all things are compounded; that there are no enduring substances that exist autonomously. According to the doctrine of dependent origination (Pratitya Samutpada) everything that exists, except the one reality of Nirvana (about which more later), depends on something else, that is, depends on an antecedent condition. Everything is a constant and changing rearrangement of basic elements of existence (skandhas). These elements or aggregates of which all things are compounded are difficult to understand but may be rendered as matter, sensation, perceptions, psychic dispositions, and consciousness. All things decay, dissolve, mutate, because the aggregates of which they are compounded, are subject to a continuous process of flux and recomposition, in response to the karmic dynamism of antecedent states. The Buddha's final words are a reminder that to live is to be involved in an inescapable process of decay and death because everything -- human life included -- is simply a rearrangement of constituent elements in a constant state of alteration. Accordingly, the intrinsic quality of life, characterized by such decay and death is correctly understood as suffering.

(b) Buddhist Meditation on Death

Buddhist meditation practices provide a dramatic reinforcement of the consciousness of death. The Buddhist aspirant is not allowed to evade or romanticize death; he is obliged to face it and to recognize its intrinsic threatening nature. In order to achieve a final state of enlightenment the disciple must normally go through preliminary stages of meditation. One of these -- called the mindfulness of death -- entails concentrating upon the reality of death.

In the Path of Purity (Visuddhimagga), the Monk Buddhaghosa instructs the monks regarding the conduct of their meditation in this manner:

"In 'the recollection of death', the word 'death' refers to the cutting off of the life-force which lasts for the length of one existence.

[The doctrine of rebirth with many existences is in the background here.] Whoso wants to develop it [referring to the recollection or mindfulness of death], should in seclusion and solitude wisely set up attention with the words: 'Death will take place, the life-force will be cut off', or (simply), 'Death, death' .... The Yogin, (the meditator) should look upon being killed or dead here and there, and advert to the death of beings who died after having first seen prosperity. To this (observation) he should apply mindfulness, perturbation and cognition, and set up attention with the words, 'Death will take place', and so on." (Conze 1972: 86-7)

Buddhaghosa goes on to say that if this seclusion and this concentration upon death, reminding oneself of its inevitability, is not enough to produce the mindfulness of death, the monk should recall death from the following eight points of view:

1. As a murderer, standing in front of him;
2. from the (inevitable) loss of (all) achievement;
3. by inference;
4. because one's body is shared with many others;

5.   from the weakness of the stuff of life;
6.   from the absence of signs;
7.   because the life-span is limited;
8.   from the shortness of the moment.

These are all meditation devices for achieving a mindfulness of death, for bringing home the truth about death. One should recall that death stands ever before us just like a murderer who confronts us with his drawn sword raised to our neck intending to cut off our head. Death is inescapable; just as one is born, one must inevitably die. Buddhaghosa then gives certain homely illustrations of the inescapability of death. First "As a budding mushroom shoots upwards carrying soil on its head, so beings from their birth onwards carry decay and death along with them. For death has come together with birth, because everyone who is born must certainly die. Therefore this being, from the time of his birth onwards, moves in the direction of death, without turning back even for a moment". (Conze 1972: 88). Another illustration: Death is inevitable, "just as the sun, once it has arisen, goes forward in the direction of its setting, and does not turn back for a moment on the path it traverses in that direction". And another: "As a mountain stream rapidly tears down on its way, flows and rushes along, without turning back even for a moment. To one who goes along like that, death is always near". Whoever seeks truth and salvation must brood upon the inexorability of death.

A second meditational device is the contemplation of the failure of achievement. There is no single worldly attainment that stands out as having transcended the threat of failure. Achievement seems worthwhile, Buddhaghosa warns, just so long as you do not contemplate the threat of its failure. But in fact that is impossible because there is no accomplishment so great as to be invulnerable. Health ends in sickness, youth in old age, all life ends in death. Wherever one may dwell in the world, one is afflicted by birth, overtaken by old age, pressed by sickness, struck down by death. The achievements of life ultimately end in the failure of death. When one realizes how evanescent are human attainments, one, at the same time, cultivates a needful mindfulness of death. Some might wish to dispute this; they might believe that some achievements share eternity, that certain works of art, for example, perdure through the ages, or that human moral attainments are stored, valued and even rewarded in some kind of eternal realm. But Buddhaghosa's argument is that all human achievements are vulnerable; the inevitability of death is the final mocker of human striving.

Buddhaghosa then speaks of recalling death 'by inference'. Here one is instructed to meditate on people -- great kings and leaders -- who have achieved fame, and then to draw the inference to oneself: death is the common lot of all. When one observes how even the distinguished die, when one notes that even their prominence affords no defence against death, then one should draw the proper conclusion with respect to one's own mortality.

Further, a monk is invited to meditate that one's body is shared with many others, animal as well as human, and shares, likewise, their common limitation and mortality. Accordingly, the Lord Buddha enjoins the following reflection: "Here, monks, a monk, when the day is over and night comes round, thinks to himself: many are, to be sure, for me the occasions of death: a snake, or a scorpion, or a centipede may bite me; thereby I may lose my life, and that may act as an obstacle (to my spiritual progress). Or I may stumble and fall, or the food I have eaten may upset me, or the bile may trouble me, or the phlegm, or the winds which cut like knives; and thereby I may lose my life, and that may act as an obstacle" (Conze 1972: 90). Meditating upon the weakness of the human body and its disposition towards multiform dangers, external and internal, induces a realization of the omnipresence of death.

Buddhaghosa mentions snakes and scorpions and centipedes -- scarcely threats that preoccupy modern Westerners. But even a brief sojourn in India's rural areas brings home the realization that these are the prospects which prompt persons there to confront their mortality. I believe that even in this day, some thirty thousand people a year die in India of snake bite. Out in the rural areas, at an ashram, for example, one does watch where the feet are placed. Especially at nighttime one is very loathe to walk across fields or through the brush lest a cobra or some other snake be disturbed and provoked to strike. Once, while visiting the temples at Khajuraho at nighttime, I stepped down from a porch in my bare feet and missed a scorpion by about an inch. The sweeper who witnessed it, just had time to yell -- as my foot hit the ground. He moved quickly to beat it with a broom and killed it. Though scorpions may not normally be lethal, they nevertheless symbolize in the Indian cultural milieu the unexpected imminence of death. For modern Westerners the most immediate mortal danger would probably be the automobile. When one recalls that approximately five thousand Canadians annually lose their lives on the highways, one might want to rewrite Buddhaghosa's exhortations to the monks to include such mechanical threats. But the central intention remains constant: by reflecting upon one's body shared with others, one comes to mindfulness of death.

Our examination of this guide for recollecting death may be brought to a close with the injunction to grasp the shortness of life. "The life-span is limited -- brief is the life of men at present; he lives long who lives for a hundred years, or a little more. Hence the Lord has said: "Short, oh monks, is the life-span of men, transient, having its sequel elsewhere; one should do what is wholesome, one should lead a holy life, no one who is born can escape death; he lives long who lives for a hundred years or a little more .... Death is surely bound to come" (Conze 1972: 92).

These meditational counsels are intended to achieve mindfulness of death. The benefits that accrue to persons who thus meditate on death, are manifold.

"The monk who is devoted to this recollection of death is always watchful, he feels disgust for all forms of becoming [that is, for this world of change], he forsakes the hankering after life, he disapproves of evil, he does not hoard up many things, and with regard to the necessities of life he is free from the taint of stinginess. He gains familiarity with the notion of impermanence, and, when he follows that up, also the notions of ill and not-self will stand out to him. At the hour of death, beings who have not developed the recollection of death feel fear, fright and bewilderment, as if they were suddenly attacked by wild beasts, ghosts, snakes, robbers or murderers. He, on the contrary, dies without fear and bewilderment. If in this very life he does not win deathlessness, he is, on the dissolution of his body, bound for a happy destiny" (Conze 1972: 94-5). (This last sentence means that even if the ultimate goal of Nirvana is not yet reached, such a monk will at least experience a good rebirth).

One of the main emphases of Buddhist meditation, we have seen, is to bring home to spiritual aspirants, as a precondition of achieving any higher goals, their own mortality. The point of this mindfulness of death is, paradoxically, to be eventually liberated from the anxiety of death. Ultimate spiritual liberation is possible only on the basis of the knowledge -- evoked by these various meditational devices -- that death is inevitable and life, therefore, distasteful. Death is a constituent and principal symbol of the sorrow that has ultimately to be transcended in the bliss of Nirvana.

To those who might think that this book is morbidly or neurotically enchanted by death, the reply is that it is in good company. By looking at the four sights, by analyzing the first of the four noble truths, by heeding the Buddha's final words, and finally by looking at some meditational practices for the recollection of death, the point has been established that in Buddhist tradition death is experienced as sorrow which has to be overcome. The Buddha's message is concerned to bring this inherent human pain to light and then to prescribe an antidote for this sorrow epitomized by death.

2. Nirvana Negatively Delineated

The Buddhist response to death is formed in a network of meanings that cluster around the term 'Nirvana'.[1] The enormous difficulty immediately faced is the declared reluctance of Buddhists to give a conceptual definition of Nirvana. This is because their theory of knowledge holds ultimate reality to be ungraspable by the names and forms -- the labels and categories -- of abstract, verbal and conceptual thinking. Moreover, attention to these philosophical questions is seen as a deflection from the crucial transformative task in which humans should properly be engaged. This explains the so-called "Silence of the Buddha" on these matters that so provoke our intellectual curiosity. This silence is illustrated by the Buddhas's position in the following parable:

A disciple, Malunkyaputta, questions him on the subject of Nirvana. Does the Tathagata ("he who has arrived at perfection") continue to live in Nirvana or is he engulfed in the Void? By way of answer, Buddha cites the

case of a man struck by a poisoned arrow.
Should he delay the treatment until he is
certain if it is a noble, a Brahmin, a Sudra,
or a slave who has wounded him? What would
be the result? The death of the wounded
man. Similarly with the man who would be
healed of Samsara. Let him content himself
then with the four Holy Truths. All else is
superfluous and runs the risk of delaying
salvation. (Henry Arvon, Buddhism: 45)

We are left with the conclusion that Nirvana can
be known only experientially or in what is sometimes
called direct mystical intuition. Conceptual knowledge
misses the realty. Thus Conze reminds us:

"Ultimately, Nirvana is unthinkable and
incomprehensible. It is only as a
therapeutically valuable, though basically
false, concept that, during certain phases of
our spiritual progress, it can be of use to
our thoughts, and enter into the practice of
contemplation" (Conze 1959: 112).

Nirvana (Sanskrit, Nirvana; Pali, Nibbana), in
spite of the claims of ineffability, is something about
which we are as students, if nothing else, obliged to
talk. Certain qualities may be predicated about
Nirvana -- the ultimate antidote to death -- though
certainly we are on more secure ground when we talk
about it in negative terms.[2]

First of all, Nirvana is liberation from
suffering. In the Buddhist analysis of existence life
is characterized by suffering; this is the first noble
truth. The Buddhist characterization of worldly
existence discloses 'the three marks of existence', as,
first of all suffering (Sanskrit, duhkha); secondly,
impermanence (Sanskrit, anitya; Pali, anicca);
soullessness (Sanskrit, anatman; Pali, anatta). The
Buddhist therapeutic answer must address itself to the
inescapable fact of suffering. Life is transmuted by
the reality of Nirvana which is that quality, state, or
condition, (all of these words are halting attempts to
say something about the unsayable) in which suffering,
sickness, senescence and death are overcome.

In the second place, Nirvana is the extinction of
desire. Von Glasenapp in Buddism: A Non-theistic
Religion (1954) says, "Nirvana is the complete and

utter dissolution of the three unwholesome roots of greed, hate and delusion." (106). Walpola Rahula says Nirvana is freedom from all evil that we have already seen, freedom from the intrinsic suffering of life, and also freedom from craving, from hating, from ignorance, and from all terms of duality. "O bhikkhus [oh monks], what is the Absolute, (unconditioned)? It is, O bhikkhus, the extinction of desire, the extinction of hatred, the extinction of illusion. This, O bhikkhus, is called the Absolute." (Rahula 1959: 36-7). The Absolute and Unconditioned are philosophical equivalents of the concept of Nirvana.

Nirvana means, thirdly, the elimination of ignorance or delusion. My interpretation of Buddhism postulates that ignorance is the fundamental flaw from which all other evils result. But precisely what is this ignorance? It is, in the first place, simply ignorance of the four noble truths. If persons do not understand that life fundamentally is suffering; if they have been bewitched by transient delights into thinking that there is substantial happiness in this life, then they are deluded and need a teacher like the enlightened one to prompt them so to reflect upon human existence as to come to see its intrinsic quality as suffering. Ignorance is, further, the failure to recognize craving as the cause of suffering. It is because life and things are desired, and because no desires can ultimately be fulfilled permanently, that human dissatisfaction and pain ensue. One craves something and does not acquire it; the consequence is suffering. Conversely, something is desired and acquired, but the consequence is still suffering because of fear of losing it. Either separation from the things desired or the fear of losing the things attained, evoke unhappiness. But, as the third noble truth declares, there is a solution to this desire-induced unhappiness. It is the cessation of craving, and entry upon nirvanic peace and bliss. Finally, there is a way that leads to Nirvana; this is the eightfold path, a way of discipline, meditation, and wisdom that brings about the cessation of craving and suffering.

But though baneful human ignorance is rightly interpreted as ignorance about the four noble truths, it entails also a failure to grasp the inherent and fundamental nature of existence. The three marks of existence, according to Buddhism, are sorrow (which we have already analysed), transiency or impermanence, and

selflessness.   Respecting impermanence, Buddhist
teaching asserts that all things are compounded. They
are in a constant state of rearrangement of certain
primary material and psychic elements of existence
called <u>skandhas</u> (Pali, <u>khandhas</u>).   This means that
there are no perduring substances in this world; there
are no things which eternally are, for everything is
constantly changing.   For example, the physical
environment of the readers has changed since they began
reading.   There   have   been   changes   --   perhaps
imperceptible -- in the light, in aging of the bricks,
in the deterioration of paint and carpetings.   There
has been, even in a short time, rearrangement of the
aggregates or components of personal existence.
Physiologically and psychologically things are
different now than when the enquiry started.   All
things are constantly in flux; everything is
impermanent.   That is one of the reasons why it is so
futile an enterprise to desire things, because desire
is normally predicated on the permanency of the desired
object, but, in fact, nothing is permanent.   All
mundane realities, inanimate and personal, are
ultimately empty of substance; their impermanence makes
them insubstantial.   To desire things is to be engaged
in a quixotic undertaking since the objects of desire
simply cannot last because, in truth, they are not.

The Buddhist analysis of existence continues with
the difficult idea of <u>anatman</u>: absence of self or
soul.   <u>Anatman</u> means literally, no-self.   The
conviction that all things are impermanent, leads
inevitably to the understanding that existence is
devoid of selves.   Normally, we think that the bricks
and carpeting in our physical setting change but that
we do not.   Granted, there are some physical and
psychological alterations that occur in the self; we
grow a bit older, acquire another grey hair or two.
But there is an essential 'me' which does not change.
Beneath all the changes which take place in our bodily
and mental existence, there is a permanent ego -- a
perduring John Smith or Mary Brown.   Or so we
frequently argue.

The Buddhists claim, however, that there is no
enduring individual self or soul.   <u>Everything</u> is in
flux.   There is no stable, unchanging personal
substance beneath the flux.   We tend to think there
is.   We do acknowledge that there is change; we know
that that tiny pink coloured baby that emerged from the
womb is quite different from the highly active two year

old, different from the delightful little child that starts off to school, different from the agitated and searching adolescent, different from youth in the height of its vigor, different from the young married, and so on, up to old age. We know there is change, but conventionally we believe, nevertheless, that beneath all those physically perceptible transient stages, there is an enduring individual substance or identity, frequently called a soul or the essential self.

This the Buddha attacks. there is no perduring individual self such as the _Gita_ suggests. The _Gita_ holds that besides the changing phenomenal self, which is not the real self, there is the eternal atman or soul. The Buddhist position is that not only is life sorrowful and transient, it is also devoid of self. But people are normally ignorant of this truth. They presume they are an enduring self, or possess an individual "I" that can desire satisfying objects. In fact, there is no individual enduring identity. Life is only a constant arrangement of the components of existence. On the basis of this ignorance of no-self, of the transiency and flux of existence, and of the fundamentally sorrowful condition of human existence, the unenlightened engage in a program which is doomed to frustration and results in sorrow.

Nirvana involves the abolition of all the negative roots of the human predicament. Because the fundamental source of human distress, including death - anxiety, is the illusion of self, Nirvana signifies, fourthly, the abolition of egoity. The Buddhist monk, Walpola Rahula, confirms this when he explains Nirvana is ultimately the annihilation of the illusion of self, of the false idea of self (Rahula 1959: 37). The aim of the Buddhist road to emancipation and Nirvana is the extinction of this false belief in a separate, individual self. Nirvana -- whatever else it is -- entails the annihilation of this illusion of separate selfhood.[3]

It is possible to grasp some of these features of life by viewing them through the lens provided by one of the dominant Buddhist symbols. The three negative human elements of desire, hatred, and ignorance, can be understood by seeing them in the context of the Buddhist wheel of life or becoming. At the very centre of the wheel of human existence, there are three mythic images. There is a rooster, a snake, and a hog. The qualities which are represented by these three images are the qualities which keep people bound to the wheel of existence. To alter the images slightly, what keeps the wheel of existence revolving is, the snake, the hog, and the cock at its hub. What qualities do they stand for? The cock or rooster stands for anger or, more generally, unbridled hostile emotion. The snake represents lechery or lust, and the hog, with its snout to the ground oblivious to the grandeur of heaven above it, represents ignorance or delusion. Nirvana is characterized negatively as the absence of these qualities. Nirvana is that transcendental condition marked by the absence of hostility and hatred, greed and lechery (which could be generically designated as craving) and ignorance and delusion. Ultimately, the condition that underlies the human predicament is delusion. It is the failure to understand the nature of existence, more specifically, the failure to grasp the selflessness of existence that generates craving and hostile emotions.

A further way of understanding Nirvana negatively, is to see it, in the fifth place, as deliverance from samsara, that is, from the wheel of rebirth and redeath. To be involved in the wheel of rebirth is to be in bondage. The wheel of samsara also entails conditions by which we are constrained, such as our social class, physical disabilities of one sort or another, or congenital weaknesses. These conditions are all part of being bound in the wheel of rebirth. The possibility of attaining Nirvana is a therapeutic answer that promises deliverance or release from the bondage of samsara and all the limitations of life.

Buddhism claims to be a vehicle which transports people across the river of samsaric existence to the shore of Nirvana. There are, traditionally, three vehicles. There is the great vehicle of the Mahayana; there is the smaller boat of the Hinayana, more correctly designated as the Theravada school; and there is the Vajrayana, the vehicle of the Thunderbolt, which is the distinctive Tibetan form of Tantric Buddhism. Buddhism is not so much conceptual truth but a practical system which transports truth seekers across the river of rebirth with its ignorance, egoity, cravings, and delusions, to the other side, to Nirvana. To enter the Buddhist vehicle, the boat of the discipline, means to begin to cross the river of life from this shore of profane life experience of non-enlightenment, the shore of spiritual ignorance, desire and death, to the yonder Nirvanic shore of transcendental wisdom, peace and bliss, which is liberation from worldly bondage.

To sum up: Nirvana is, negatively speaking, the cessation of suffering; it is the extinction of desire and the elimination of suffering and desire's root cause -- ignorance; it is freedom from egoity and duality; and, finally, it is deliverance from the wheel of rebirth, from samsaric existence of bondage and limitation.

There is a distinction made between Nirvana achieved in this body, and Nirvana after death. Nirvana achieved during this life while still in one's body is called Nirvana with the skandhas. Nirvana achieved without the skandhas after death is the parinirvana or great Nirvana. Siddartha Gautama, for example, achieved enlightenment or Buddhahood under the bodi tree following long weeks of meditation. Thereupon, he entered Nirvana. But because he remained behind to preach for forty-five years for the benefit of mankind, he delayed entry into the final Nirvana until his death at age eighty. He entered Nirvana at age thirty-five at the time of enlightenment, but he did not enter the plenitude of Nirvana -- the great Nirvana -- until his death.

It must be noted that Nirvana is not heaven. According to the Buddhist cosmology, heavens do exist in which one may spend a pleasant respite from samsara in the presence of deities. But even heavens are ultimately under the suzerainty of samsara -- the wheel of existence characterized by death and suffering.

3. Death, Selflessness and Nirvana

Death is experienced as dread by the unenlightened because their perception is characterized by differentiation. Centrally, that means the mistaken move that separates out the ego from the non-ego. Having committed this fundamental error, the problem is compounded by desiring life, power and benefits for this individual self or ego. The consequence is suffering. For once life is defined in terms of separate self, and happiness is defined in terms of gratification of this separate self's desires, a hopeless situation has been created. For the nature of existence is such that the ego's desires can never be fully or adequately met. The attempt to do so results in frantic, though ultimately vain, activity.

Liberation from the dread of death comes only when enlightenment dawns that there is, in reality, no separate self such as could crave life and tremble at the prospect of its own extinction.

That is the Buddhist therapy. There is no self such as could be extinguished and engender death anxiety. Apprehension comes only to the unenlightened. Once the Buddhist coping mechanism -- the doctrine of <u>anatman</u> and Nirvana has been internalized, then this perturbation vanishes.

Worldly, historical existence of humans is to be understood as a phenomenal flux whose components are in a constant state of rearrangement throughout what is perceived as unitary life. Such an identity is in fact, a constant rearrangement of elements that goes on throughout life and continues at the point that is perceived as death. What happens at death when the body dies, is only a dramatic instance of what has been going on throughout life, namely constant reassembly of the <u>skandhas</u> or elements of existence. During life, this process of decomposition and recomposition is not so noticeable; at death, the rearrangement of aggregates is quite dramatic. But in life, as at death, there is no eternal individual self or enduring ego that underlies the constant recomposition of the phenomenal constituents of existence.

Beyond the impermanency of mundane existence there is the undifferentiated bliss of Nirvana -- a transcendent quality about which nothing can be said except heuristically. But there is no individual self who can die.

Because I have adopted a negative way in attempting to delineate Nirvana, there is a danger that this vibrant, positive insight into Nirvana as bliss may be obscured. Let me correct the imbalance by including a passage that points to the serenity and joy of those who have transcended all anxieties of routine, phenomenal existence:

> He who has realized the Truth, Nirvana, is the happiest being in the world. He is free from all 'complexes' and obsessions, the worries and troubles that torment others. His mental health is perfect. He does not repent the past, nor does he brood over the future. He lives fully in the present.

Therefore he appreciates and enjoys things in the purest sense without self-projections. He is joyful, exultant, enjoying the pure life, his faculties pleased, free from anxiety, serene and peaceful. As he is free from selfish desire, hatred, ignorance, conceit, pride, and all such 'defilements', he is pure and gentle, full of universal love, compassion, kindness, sympathy, understanding and tolerance. His service to others is of the purest, for he has no thought of self. He gains nothing, accumulates nothing, not even anything spiritual, because he is free from the illusion of Self, and the 'thirst' for becoming. (Rahula 1959: 43)

The Buddhist therapeutic answer to death may be put another way. Death ought not to provoke dread and anxiety for there is not, in reality, any death. If death be taken to mean the dissolution of an individual ego, then there can be no death because there is no individual self.

There is, of course, change and decay on the phenomenal level which provides the perceptible data for the conclusion -- false, as we have seen -- that death exists. But what is called death is in reality, the rearrangement of skandhas -- the physical and psychical aggregrates of phenomenal existence. The reason this rearrangement has been conceived as death, and feared, is because ignorance has generated a delusion of an enduring separate ego that underlies these phenomenal changes.

The radical soteriological aim of classical Buddhism seems, however, psychologically difficult to maintain in the piety of the masses. Just as in Christian tradition there is a shift from resurrection of the body to immortality of the soul, so in Buddhist tradition we perceive a shift in certain quarters from what Melford Spiro, in his analysis of Burmese Buddhists, calls nibbanic Buddhism to kammatic Buddhism. The soteriological goal shifts from Nirvana to the achievement of good Karma through meritorious deeds and a subsequent pleasant rebirth. This shift is correlated with a replacement of the doctrine of anatta-(nonself) by that of a 'butterfly' spirit or soul that justifies a moral scheme of action and its appropriate punishments or rewards in the next rebirth.

1. This is R.C. Amore's view of the Buddhist response
    to death. He says boldly: "The answer to death
    is Nirvana, the state of deathlessness." (Amore
    1974: 127).

2. Even this way of negative characterization is
    ultimately false. It does, however, have a
    provisional, heuristic value, that is, it can be
    instrumental in bringing about true understanding
    even if in itself it is untrue. In this regard we
    may note the following:

    > To speak seriously, therefore, of
    > nirvana as a goal to be attained
    > is simply to betray the
    > attitude of one still remembering
    > or experiencing the process as
    > the burning of the fire. The
    > Buddha himself adopts such
    > an attitude only for the teaching of
    > those still suffering, who feel
    > that they would like to make the
    > flames extinct. His famous Fire
    > Sermon is an accommodation, not
    > by any means the final word of
    > the sage whose final word is
    > silence. From the perspective of
    > the Awake, the Illumined One,
    > such opposed verbalizations as
    > nirvana and samsara,
    > enlightenment and ignorance,
    > freedom and bondage, are without
    > reference, void of content. That
    > is why the Buddha refused to
    > discuss nirvana. (Zimmer 1956:
    > 480).

3. Cf., "There are many roads to emancipation. What
    is common to all of them is that they aim at the
    extinction of the belief in individuality."
    (Conze 1959: 13).

REFERENCES

Amore, R.C.
1974 "The Heterodox Philosophical Systems" in
Frederick H. Holck, ed., Death and Eastern
Thought. Nashville: Abingdon.

Conze, Edward
1972 Buddhist Meditation. London: Unwin Books.
First published in the Ethical and Religious
Classics of East and West series in 1956.

1959 Buddhism: Its Essence and Development. New
York: Harper Torchbooks.

Glasenapp, Helmuth Von
1954 Buddhism: A Non-Theistic Religion. New
York: George Braziller.

Rahula, Walpola
1959 What the Buddha Taught. New York: Grove
Press.

Spiro, Melford E.
1972 Buddhism and Society: A great Tradition and
its Burmese Vicissitudes. New York: Harper &
Row (Paperbacks).

Zimmer, Heinrich
1956 Philosophies of India, New York: Meridian
Books.

CHAPTER EIGHT

SECULARIZATION'S IMPACT ON ATTITUDES TO DEATH

1. Alteration of Religious Outlooks

Secular world views are largely (though not exclusively) the consequence of science and technology: science that delivers naturalistic interpretations of events in the place of supernatural causation; technology which places ever greater control over nature and events in the hands of humans. Thus purged of helplessness in the face of uncontrolled, superior forces, mankind has less and less need to resort to Gods for help.

The effect of secularization is to break the official religious cosmos; to destroy traditional conceptions of an underlying order and meaning which supplies hope and therapy for religious persons who have experienced contradiction and impotence in the face of death. To secularized persons religious doctrines of the afterlife may seem like fairytales or science fiction.

By challenging a society's official religious tradition, secularism also heightens the note of personal choice in appropriating an interpretation of death. Peter Berger, in The Sacred Canopy (1969), has pointed out that secularization affects not only consciousness by shattering the unquestioned stability of the religious cosmos; it also has social repercussions.

The cosmological monopoly previously held by traditional religious institutions is challenged and eventually abolished. The consequence is a pluralistic situation with various social bodies offering contending soteriological options. Secularism itself may represent an implicit world view in competition with other conventional religious constructions of reality. No longer is the worldview articulated by the official custodians of a religious tradition taken for granted. From being presupposed, their world-view becomes one among a number of possible interpretations. Now a conscious choice is forced upon the person who seeks an integrated cosmological perspective and soteriological program.

We must, however, bear in mind that secularized

cosmologies which replace traditional religious ones
may still generate such a sense of cosmic value and
meaning as to mitigate the tragic reaction to
mortality. Faith in a moral universe which justifies
the pursuit of certain noble values in life, and
guarantees the eternity of such qualities, could
readily function in a therapeutic way. Here we may
recall Kubler-Ross' finding that atheists may reach
acceptance of death equally with religious persons.

2. Naturalism and Death

Evidence of secularization may be seen in the
prominence of naturalistic themes in modern
literature. Naturalism declares man to be continuous
with nature. He may be viewed biologically as an
animal driven by genetically programed appetites and
instincts, or as matter determined by physical forces
and chemical elements.

When man's animal nature is stressed we have
Darwinism -- the law of life is the struggle for
existence in which the fittest (those best adapted to
the environment) survive according to natural
selection. This is exemplified by the protagonist in
Dreiser's The Financier who visits a fish market daily
to see the lobster vanquish the squid. This is the
paradigm for his own life and his success in the
context of the business world.

When matter is stressed, we have mechanism -- man
functions like a machine in a greater machine, subject
to the same material forces as all other material
things. There is no autonomous spirit or sovereign
free will. When the machine breaks down in death that
is the end of man. This outlook is set out by the
American novelist Theodore Dreiser:

> Of one's ideals, struggles,
> deprivations, sorrows and joys, it could
> only be said that they were chemical
> compulsions, something which for some
> inexplicable but unimportant reason
> responded to and resulted from the hope
> of pleasure and the fear of pain. Man
> was a mechanism, undevised and
> uncreated, and a badly and carelessly
> driven one at that. (cited in Killinger
> 1968:143)

- 128 -

Even a naturalistic interpretation of life and death, however, may still function with a worldview, or perspective that makes death intelligible, even if that stance be the harsh one of survival of the fittest in the evolutionary process of nature.

In fact, Darwinian naturalism may be viewed in a highly optimistic way as an explanatory justification for the belief in the world's creative evolutionary progress. It is only through death according to nature's selective process that evolutionary advance is possible. Were there no death, the unfit, the weak, the less complex, the less adaptable species would co-exist with the fit, making human evolution impossible. This assessment still finds its articulate supporters:

> In a larger and deeper sense, every human death is ultimately for the good of the group. It is, at least in biological terms, the most fundamental of creative acts ... It is scarcely necessary to review all the facts that attest to the role of selective death in the evolutionary process. It must be equally, or perhaps even more, obvious that cultural evolution also relies on death not only to select the "fittest", but simply to make room and to give more opportunity for the bearers of new ideas and novel life styles. If Ponce de Leon and his colleagues had ever found the Fountain of Eternal Youth, it would have soon shown itself a pool of stagnation. (Morison 1975: 99-100).

Camus' wry observation may be pertinent here: "A world that can be explained even with bad reasons is a familiar world." (The Myth of Sisyphus, 5). The drive for lucidity and consolation may indeed seduce us into a premature acquiesence in doubtful arguments.

3. Contemporary Existentialism And Death

In a pre-secular period of consciousness, as we have noted, official religious cosmologies tended to be presupposed. The devotees of a tradition inhabited a more or less stable and objective world. Human struggles to overcome sin, ignorance, the effects of tabu violation or death were undoubtedly present, but these soteriological efforts were acted out against the backdrop of a communally defined and accepted world order.

But the modern question is: Does the evidence of life support any meaning or validate any ultimate value? What if all worldviews or cosmologies are called into question? What if Nietzsche's proclamation of the death of God and its attendant nihilism should carry the day? It must be remembered that the declaration of the death of God signifies not only the rejection of all theistic interpretations of the universe which underlie answers to death (like resurrection of the body), but also all claims to a metaphysical reality or order underlying the world of appearance. Nietzsche's nihilism implies there is no Nirvana, no immortal soul, no transcendent realm of Platonic pure ideas, no purposive historical process. Such a nihilistic view of things appears to deprive its adherents of any basis for hope; to cling to a view of life and reality that affords a therapy for the pain and problematic of death is, on nihilistic premises, an illusory activity. One of the virtues claimed for the existentialist analysis of human existence is precisely that it seeks to proceed without any illusions, deceptions or lies; the dissolution of the matter-of-factness of the official cosmos is defiantly accepted. The existentialist approach takes for granted that a meaning for life cannot simply be read off the universe as it confronts us. There are no rationally compelling data that either oblige us to acquiesce in such meaning, or reassure us that a cosmic meaning is palpably the case. Reality is no longer something clearly and objectively given; it must be discovered, if at all, in a conative quest arising out of human freedom. Kierkegaard's epigram "Truth is subjectivity" means that the sacred cosmos -- the real world - is not delivered by religious institutional authority nor by detached, objective reasoning. Rather, if a reality other than fragmentary chaos exists, it must be apprehended in a subjective act of total engagement.

An instance of such analysis may be seen in Camus' The Plague (1947) where the plague and quarantining of the city of Oran in Algeria are presented as symbols of life as it is initially encountered. In Camus' earlier

(1942) theoretical work, The Myth of Sisyphus, life is seen under the symbol of "the midst of the desert". In The Plague the existentialist analysis of human situation is sketched out in recurring themes of exile, separation, despondency, prison-house, fear, suffering, despair. All this is summed up in the symbol of the plague. "What's natural is the microbe" (107). The quarantining of Oran is also a parable of human existence; it is alienation. Camus declares in The Myth of Sisyphus that it is precisely in the experience of "divorce between man and his life; the actor and his setting" that one knows the poignancy and tragic quality of life.

The sense of absurdity is generated, in part, by the specific facts of modern existence; it is a period which in fifty years has uprooted, enslaved or killed 70 million human beings. Gil Elliot's Twentieth Century Book of the Dead catalogues the specific peoples and places over which death has reigned in our time. But in the background is the general reality of human mortality. As we saw in Tillich's existential analysis, this threat of fate and death provides the constant context for human anxiety.

This is the vision of the world characterized by atheistic existentialists like Camus, as absurd. As he says: "In a universe suddenly divested of illusions and lights, man feels an alien, a stranger." (The Myth of Sisyphus, 5).

If this analysis is correct, if life has no evident intrinsic meaning, no immediately discernible order, in which our death can find a place, what follows? In the face of this, various possibilities suggest themselves:

(1) Cynicism and opportunism. This attitude is exemplified by Cottard, the gangster in The Plague, who uses the crisis of the epidemic to shield himself from capture and to profiteer from others' misery.

(2) Nihilism. This leads logically to suicide, which is the theme of The Myth of Sisyphus.

(3) Religious leaps of faith. In The Plague, the religious leap of faith is epitomized by Father Paneloux for whom suffering and death are divine chastisement.

(4) <u>Humanitarian atheism</u>. Dr. Rieux and Tarrou personify the thesis already reached abstractly in <u>The Myth of Sisyphus</u>, viz., "suicide is not legitimate"; "it is possible to find the means to proceed beyond nihilism"; "to live and create in the midst of the desert". Without God, without any metaphysical supports, one can yet commit oneself to the relief of the plague's victims, to the struggle against suffering and death, especially the death of the innocent.

On the surface, it appears that an atheistic existentialism like Camus' suffers double jeopardy. It acknowledges the opaqueness of experience respecting an underlying metaphysical order and value. Human experience of the world is, at best, ambiguous, and, at worst, downright absurd. Consequently, no meaning such as might reassure an anxious humanity can be logically extrapolated from our experience of the world. But to compound despair, subjective leaps of faith are repudiated as manifestations of weakness or bad faith. Suicide might indeed seem a logical course of action.

An yet it is not at all evident that Camus' heroic characters escape the recourse to a leap of faith. Admittedly, it is not made in terms of traditional theological cosmologies like Father Panaloux's. Nevertheless, Dr. Rieux's and Tarrou's resolution to expend their lives in selfless alleviation of human suffering do point to a decision to espouse the value of love and service rather than narcissism and cynicism. Granted, this atheistic leap of faith differs from conventional religious commitments in that it does not ground its valuation and conduct in an ontology. Otherwise, the psychological dynamics of a rationally unsubstantiated commitment -- a leap of faith -- appear the same.

One may decide that Father Paneloux's direction is mistaken; that he erred in his discernment of the world's intrinsic character and of the values and way of life compatible with it. One might well want to leap other than the way in which he did. But in the absence of invulnerable rational evidence of cosmic structure, meaning and value, leap one must. One can initially only hope that the clues to which one responds in passionate commitment are symptomatic of reality as it truly is. With good fortune, one may subsequently enjoy a subjective certitude about the correctness of one's leap of faith. Secularists, especially of a positivist scientific bent, may

continue to insist that religious interpretations of
death and afterlife amount to nothing more than
fanciful, and even immoral, inventions of the human
imagination. Theological leaps of faith like Father
Paneloux's or the devotees of other religions, are
disdained. The apparently competing views promulgated
by the various religious traditions all seem equally
incapable of verification, and hence share the
unsubstantiality of fables and wish fulfillment. This
dissatisfaction with traditional religious views
explains why there is today a heightened interest in
the findings of para-psychology and transpersonal
psychology. By this means, it is hoped, the question
of what happens after death may receive an answer not
dependent on archaic religious presuppositions or
imaginative flights from anxiety, but on the publicly
verifiable data and inference produced by scientific
method. We observed earlier that the atheistic
existentialism of Camus demands the rejection of
religious leaps of faith as bad faith. Now it must be
recognized that generally the existentialist position
also represents a reaction against scientific
determinism and the presumption of objective
explanations of human behaviour implied in scientific
perspectives on death and afterlife.

Existentialism rejects the view that human destiny
is the result of coercive naturalistic forces that
ordain that things must be as they are and no other
way. In opposition to this, it affirms the reality of
human freedom -- a freedom that opens possibilities of
personal attainment that transcend the limitations of
natural conditions and scientific knowledge.

Moreover, such scientism often represents a
failure to understand the nature of religious symbols
and myths. They should not, I have argued throughout,
be dismissed out of hand as absurd or unsubstantiated
fantasies; they represent in their appeal to the
imagination, putative insights into the nature of life.
Religious symbols (in the broadest sense) are
expressions of the meaning and value of, or in, life as
this has been discovered by the religious communities
which live in terms of those symbols. Their outlooks
on death and the afterlife are really implications of
their views on life and its highest values and goals.

This position we noted earlier in the existential
hermeneutic of the resurrection of the body. The
Christian, for example, in the last analysis, believes

in the resurrection of the body because he has an antecedent conviction about the character of God which makes final annihilation in death impossible. The vision of the loving Father who creates and controls life is incompatible with the prospect of final and eternal alienation from that Father's love.

Attitudes on death or views about the afterlife derive ultimately from the existential decision and commitment one has made in response to life's ambiguities and to a summons to transformation encountered in the midst of human crisis. Normally, one has first a faith about life; the attitude or faith about death comes after and depends on it. Or, in other words, one's assessment about the meaning of death and hope for afterlife is the result of the experiential leap of faith taken during life in defiance of perceived contradictions.

The analysis, in a succeeding chapter, of the role of faith in reaching acceptance of death illustrates the connection between the meaning of life and the meaning of death. There I argue that the person, who in the face of ambiguous or even contradictory evidence, commits and opens himself to ultimate soteriological transformation, to genuine awareness and love, is thereby endowed with an abundant sense of self-worth, integrity and acceptance that cannot be abolished even by the power of death.

4. Suicide

I want to make some concluding comments about existentialism and shall use these to illumine a few observations about suicide.

The world, it has been said, is experienced as chaos. Chaos is used here as a very general symbolic term to mean a world awry -- a world characterized by the threat of meaninglessness or uninterpretability, the threat of guilt, the threat of disproportional suffering, and death. Chaos is a symbol for a world of negative and destructive conditions. The religious answer is to make a leap of faith that says in spite of chaos, or beyond chaos, there is a sacred cosmos. Cosmos means an ordered existence. There is an admission that the empirical world (at least as initially perceived), does have those negative characteristics catalogued above. The religious message declares, however, there is another dimension, within or beyond this world, that is the true world. Life ought to be lived in conformity with that sacred cosmos which the tradition discloses to its devotees.

Atheistic existentialism, as exemplified by Camus, has the same starting point -- chaos -- but finds itself unable to make the leap of faith that discovers beyond chaos another, better, orderly world. We are stuck with chaos exemplified basically by death; there is no sacred cosmos. This threatening chaos cannot be transformed into a consoling cosmos.

In Camus' The Myth of Sisyphus the problem of suicide is examined in detail. If life is absurd -- rationally and morally -- or, to phrase it in a now familiar way, meaningless, is suicide the logical inference to draw? "Does its [existence's] absurdity require one to escape it through hope or suicide -- that is what must be clarified ... Does the Absurd dictate death?" (Camus 1955: 7). Durkheim, in Suicide, had earlier drawn the connection between meaninglessness and self-destruction. He had distinguished egoistic suicide which is the result of an individual's failure to integrate into society and live by its standards, and anomic suicide which is the result of a social breakdown in which agreed norms and values disappear.

Camus had decided against suicide even in a world which is anomic, that is, absurd or meaningless. For a humanitarian existentialist like Camus suicide is rejected in favour of the courage to be.

In the face of chaos, Camus' answer is heroism -- a defiant acknowledgement of the nihilistic character of this world as being devoid of pattern, providential will, or an undergirding Father's love. But rather than capitulating to pessimism, and even suicide, one can adopt a defiant, heroic attitude and live in terms of life projects, life goals, for which there is no metaphysical support, but which one freely chooses to espouse.

Most religious traditions, however, have prohibited suicide for explicit theological reasons given in sacred writings like the Torah, Qur'an, or Vedas. Generally, such theological reasons involve the presentation of a sacred cosmos within which human life has meaning and direction over against the threat of

meaningless and aimlessness. However, even within the
religious traditions there is a recognition of special
circumstances that justify taking one's life. Hence we
have the endorsement of such practices as <u>suttee</u> (the
self-immolation of widows on their husband's funeral
pyre) in Hinduism; <u>hara-kiri</u> in Shinto; and martyrdom
in Christianity.

Theological reasons, found in Christian tradition
(probably in the Jewish and Muslim as well), which
ground the prohibition on suicide are usually as
follows:

(1) Explicit divine prohibition forbidding killing
or murder -- "Thou shalt not kill".

(2) God's custodial or property rights over the
lives of his creatures. Killing the self denies the
<u>sovereignty</u> of the Creator of life who alone can
appoint its length and end.

(3) God's providential guidance and care which
would be denied by resorting to suicide in adversity.

(4) The salutary chastisement and challenge of
suffering.

The question: Are there any circumstances in
which suicide is ever morally right? receives another
sort of answer in the type of suicide characterized by
Durkheim as 'altruistic'. Examples of such altruistic
suicide may be observed in:

-The exit of the frost-incapacitated Titus Oates,
from the tent into the Antarctic blizzard to
relieve Scott and his companions of the delaying
burden caused by frozen feet, during the tragic
and ultimately fatal return of the British
expedition from the South Pole in 1912.

-The aged Inuit grandmother in Farley Mowat's
<u>People of the Deer</u>, who surrenders herself to
death in the Arctic night rather than continue a
non-productive drain on the scarce food supply.

- Certain hypothetical cases in Bonhoeffer's <u>Ethics</u>.

These instances are not egoistic suicide which is
the result of personal guilt at the loss of meaning and
value. Nor are they anomic suicide which is the result

of social or cosmic meaninglessness or normlessness.
Rather, such cases of suicide are altruistic, that is,
self-destruction for the sake of the well-being of
others.

REFERENCES

Berger, Peter
    1969 <u>The Sacred Canopy: Elements of a Sociological Theory of Religion</u>. Garden City, New York: Doubleday Anchor Books.

Camus, Albert
    1955 <u>The Myth of Sisyphus</u>. New York: Vintage Books. <u>Le Mythe de Sisyphe</u> first published in 1942.

    1960 <u>The Plague</u>. Harmondsworth: Penguin Books. <u>La Peste</u> first published in 1947.

Durkheim, Emile
    1952 <u>Suicide</u>. Translated by J.A. Spaulding and G. Simpson. London: Routledge & Kegan Paul.

Elliot, Gil
    1973 <u>Twentieth Century Book of the Dead</u>. Harmondsworth: Penguin Books.

Killinger, James
    1969 "Death and Transcendence in Contemporary Literature" in Liston O. Mills, ed., <u>Perspectives on Death</u>. Nashville: Abingdon Press.

Morison, Robert S.
    1975 "The Dignity of the Inevitable and Necessary" in Peter Steinfels and Robert M. Veatch, <u>Death Inside Out</u>. New York: Harper & Row.

CHAPTER NINE

THE ROLE OF FAITH AND BELIEF IN FACING DEATH

I want to deal now with the respective roles of belief and faith in facing death. Having completed our exploration of religions as therapies for death we must beware a grave misunderstanding of an ideational sort. It would be a mistake to suppose that the coping mechanisms proffered by religious traditions consist in the transmission and inculcation of certain ideas. It is entirely intelligible that this mistaken inference should be drawn because the very process of making an intellectual presentation such as the present one risks speaking of religious therapies for death as if they entailed mainly the internalization of ideas. We have, for example, seen that Hebraic tradition teaches that the existential anxiety of death may be countered by relying on the corporate solidarity which endures even when the individual dies. The impression might be conveyed that consolation and triumph come simply by adhering with the mind to the idea that my group, my nation, my people, my collectivity will go on after my death. Similarly, the inference may have been drawn that other religious cultures such as those of the Gita or Phaedo require that, in the face of death, the devotee cling to the idea of the immortal soul, saying, 'My eternal soul will not perish, though my body dissolve'. The conviction might readily have been garnered that the way various religious traditions deal with the dread of death, is by encouraging their adherents to espouse or give mental assent to certain therapeutic or redemptive ideas. But I hasten to correct that misapprehension. As far as I can tell, the religious way of meeting death does not consist only, or mainly, possibly not even at all, of appropriating religious ideas as such. This is particularly paradoxical to intellectuals who are trained to feel that the incorporation of ideas into the network of their thinking is what constitutes the important matter in life. Such conceptual analysts are inclined to think that the decisive question to ask of any tradition they are trying to understand is, "What do they believe". It is a widespread assumption that we understand things like religious traditions by grasping their conceptual or doctrinal content. But we err if we approach the matter so simply.

Essential to grasping the dynamics of religious transformation is an understanding of the distinction

between belief and faith. Believing and having faith
are two forms of being religious, one of which is
efficacious in dealing with the anxiety of death, and
the other not. Believing, by which I mean basically,
adhering with the mind to ideas, is not effective in
handling the threat of death. The other modality of
religiousness -- having faith, i.e., trusting
committedly the tradition's transcendent power -- is.
I want to elucidate this distinction between belief and
faith as diverse ways of responding to death by drawing
upon insights from Elizabeth Kubler-Ross and Wilfred
Cantwell Smith whose work, though starting from highly
divergent directions, converges in their shared
conviction about the centrality of faith.

1. Religion and Acceptance of Death in Kubler-Ross

There are in Kubler-Ross suggestions that in
meeting death adequately -- on her premises this means
winning through to a stage of acceptance beyond denial,
rage, bargaining, and despair -- it is not so much
specific religious ideas that are significant, but the
act of faith itself. In this regard, she says, "The
significant variable is not the what of faith, but the
how of it -- whether the ideas are intensely and
authentically held or internalized."[1] This finding
has important ramifications for grasping the connection
between religion and the experience of, and response
to, death on a level more deep and mysterious than the
purely ideational level.

An analysis of certain contrasts contained in
questions addressed to Kubler-Ross illumine her
judgement about the role of religious conceptions and
religious faith in dying well. In responding to these
questions, Kubler-Ross contrasts several groups of
persons and their respective responses to dying --
especially their relative ability to arrive at the
final stage of acceptance. A sketch of these five sets
of contrasting groups follows.

(1) Religious Patients vs. Non-Religious Patients

Question: "Will a person with a firm belief in his
religion ... go through these same stages of dying?"

On the basis of her clinical experience,
Kubler-Ross concluded that religious persons die
better, i.e., with greater acceptance of human finitude

and limitation. She states, "Religious people also go through the same stages of dying, but quicker and with less turmoil". Also, "Truly religious people with a deep abiding relationship with God have found it much easier to face death with equanimity". Non-religious persons, on the contrary, with the exception of convinced atheists, do not reach the peace and serenity of acceptance so readily.

Although Kubler-Ross' response to this question attests the therapeutic advantage of being religious, it contains no elaboration of what it means to be religious. The following contrasts provide some insight into the nature of that religiousness which is of critical significance at the time of dying.

(2) Religious Persons vs. Atheists

Question: "Have you dealt with an atheist and how did he or she accept death?"

Both religious and atheistic persons show the same degree of acceptance in the face of death. Kubler-Ross has worked, admittedly, with relatively few of either category. The authentically and intensely religious do not normally come within her purview because they do not normally require psychiatric consultation. The atheist, like the deeply religious person, seems to share a convinced belief in a coherent interpretation of the universe that bestows meaning on his life, i.e., generates an acceptable relation with the cosmic order and its highest value.

The initial presumption here is that a convinced and dedicated atheist has a belief system (though obviously a differing one than the theist) that can be authentically internalized, i.e., genuinely held, so as to enable an easier, accepted, dying.

(3) Christian Patients vs. Non-Christian Patients

Question: "In your work with the dying patient, have you noticed a difference between the Christian dying patient and the non-Christian as to how they accept death?"

Both groups, Kubler-Ross discovers, attain the final stage of acceptance equally well, in spite of their differing belief systems.

Christian faith does not seem to provide an advantage over non-Christian faith though, if truly held or internalized, it is an advantageous factor over the absence of faith. But the same judgement can be made about the positive advantage (i.e., acceptance-gaining function) of non-Christian faith over the absence of faith.

(4) Persons Who Possess a Specific Idea of Immortality vs. Those Who Do Not

Question: "Do people who do not have a concept of immortality have a harder time working through the different stages?"

Kubler-Ross' finding in this respect is that "it does not matter whether your religious belief includes a specific belief in immortality. It is more relevant that whatever you are, whatever religious beliefs you have, you are genuine and authentic".

(5) Intensely Religious vs. Nominally Religious

Question: "In your experience, do intensely religious people accept death more easily than most others?"

Kubler-Ross' inference here is that, "Truly religious people with a deep abiding relationship with God have found it much easier to face death with equanimity. We do not often see them because they aren't troubled, so they don't need our help".

The genuinely religious meet death in an easier, more serene way. The nominally religious -- 95% of Kubler-Ross' patients -- have difficulties, and benefit from counselling. "They have the additional concern about punishment after death, regrets and guilt about missed opportunities". Here we see that both groups -- the intensely religious and the nominally so -- hold the same ideas, but have a different faith, that is, a different subjective quality of integration and commitment.

Summary and Thesis

The first contrast indicates that truly religious persons reach acceptance in the face of death more readily than non-religious persons. The second, third and fourth contrasts indicate that persons with different belief systems, i.e., different ideas about reality, attain the same end, namely, the peace and detachment of the acceptance stage in dying.

These contrasts suggest two possible conclusions: First, that beliefs are extraneous to the human quality of acceptance. Second, that differing ideas -- when authentically internalized -- can function therapeutically in a similar way. It is this construction that Kubler-Ross espouses, stressing the existential element of whole-hearted commitment to the beliefs in question.

The fifth contrast (between the intensely and nominally religious) reinforces the centrality of this commissive dimension, for it brings to light the phenomenon of two groups holding the same beliefs but holding them in a qualitatively different way. One holds them in a manner that shapes their personal faith, their basic orientation, outlooks and values in life. The other holds them superficially so that this latter group's attitudes, valuations and conduct are not integrally connected with their beliefs. Here, again, though the role of beliefs is not dismissed it is the transformational quality of their sincere internalization that is stressed.

The chief inference to be drawn from all this is that the kind of religiousness that is of significance in dealing therapeutically with death is not mental assent or external adherence to certain ideas about God, man and afterlife. Rather, it is faith. It is the quality of being committed in a single-minded way to whatever is experienced as supremely real and worthy and hence authoritative over one's life. To the amplification of this thesis involving a contrast between non-therapeutic 'belief' and efficacious 'faith' we now turn.

2. Belief and Faith in Wilfred Cantwell Smith

In arriving at an understanding of the kind of religiousness that matters in reaching acceptance of death, I have found Wilfred Cantwell Smith's analysis of belief and faith highly illuminating. To put his contribution succinctly, it could be said that Smith tells us why 'belief' is largely ineffective in dying well. In what follows I detail certain features of Smith's thought in his Belief and History that pertain to this problem.

Smith's principal thesis is that there has occurred a major change in the western understanding of what it means to be religious and that this transmutation is reflected in the changing meaning of the terms 'belief' and 'believing'. He explains his findings this way:

> It can be demonstrated that the very notion of believing has itself been changing, drastically. Specifically in our case, the English word "believe" has, in usage, connotation, and denotation, undergone an arresting transformation. The change seems to have taken place unnoticed, so that a major new development in religious history has happened, as it were, casually. The shift has been a transition from a concern with something else to a concern with belief. The process has been evinced in the form of a massive shift in meaning of a word ... The word "believing" has persisted; but its meaning and usage have changed. (Smith 1977: 40)

Smith's method in establishing this thesis is a thorough word study that ranges through medieval texts, Francis Bacon, Hobbes, Locke, Shakespeare, John Stuart Mill and modern linguistic analysis. A penetrating analysis of biblical terms and concepts leads to the conclusion that belief (in the modern sense) is non-scriptural.

Smith's research discloses that 'believing' has come to mean a mental action:

(1)   whose object is a proposition
(2)   whose subject is usually a third person
(3)   which is associated with dubiousness
       concerning the belief asserted.

This understanding of belief represents a radical, recent shift in meaning.

In earlier periods of western intellectual history, starting with the Medieval period, believing meant:

(1)   a pledging of loyalty to a person (cf. credo: I give my heart)

(2) an action which was self-involving, (i.e., involves principally oneself as the subject of the believing)

(3) a commitment of oneself to that which one knew or recognized to be true.

Because, 'believing' at one time did mean 'having faith', the prevalence of this word in Christian language is readily accounted for. It is a legacy of its original meaning. As Smith says, "The word 'belief' used to be central for Christians when it designated something else" (69). The wide occurrence of 'believing' is further explained when it is recognized that there is in English no verb cognate with faith, as in other languages, and the use of 'believe' was precisely to render this sense of 'having faith', i.e., committing oneself with one's whole life to whatever was acknowledged as supremely real and worthy.

It should be borne in mind that what we observe here is not only a shift in the meaning of a word but a far-reaching transformation of the nature of religiousness, of which the semantic change of 'belief' is only a symptom. If it be true, though, that words normally carry with them the metaphysical context which gives them a semantic location, then the damaging consequences of 'believing' as one's principal religious activity may be fairly readily perceived.

If believe now means (as I contend Smith has established) to adhere with tentativeness -- even with a sense of probable falsity -- to a proposition, then the devotee who approaches his religious tradition with the believing mode of consciousness is precluded from that total personal self-surrender to a reality acknowledged as supremely true and which in turn releases transformative and therapeutic power into his life. Instead, his mental framework is one of half-hearted (rather than single-minded) attachment to religious entities understood basically as abstract propositions, and of whose truth he harbours reservations in any case. It is reasonable to doubt that such a religious attitude could possibly contribute to that buoyancy of spirit, cosmic confidence, and personal acceptance that makes dying tolerable.

In sum, to pose the question of the role of

religion in reaching acceptance of death in terms of
belief will, from the outset, determine a largely
negative answer. Believing certain doctrines about
God, or afterlife, will be a futile therapy for the
anxiety of death. First, because the object of belief
is an abstraction, an idea about a Supreme being or
transmundane life, and secondly, because believing it
assumes a provisionalness of attitude that reflects the
secularization of consciousness in modern times.

3. Ideas and the Object of Faith

If it is not believing that constitutes that
religious quality of life within which it is possible
to triumph over death, what is it? Kubler-Ross, as we
noted at the beginning, discerns that the significant
variable in reaching acceptance of death is not the
mere possession of certain beliefs but rather a certain
existential quality of commitment and authenticity.
Smith, we also observed, is convinced on the basis of
his historical researches and his personal and
comparativist experience, that the fundamental
religious quality and category has been and -- to the
extent that religiousness retains authentic connection
with its traditions -- remains, 'faith'.

Now that the commonly held sense of believing has
become the possession "of dubious, or at best
problematic, propositions" (Smith 1977: 69), to relate
oneself to religious realities according to the
modality of believing, is to condemn oneself to a
truncated, attenuated and inefficacious religious
life. It is only when religiousness retains the
characteristics of "allegiance, loyalty, integrity,
love, commitment, trust and entrusting ... in short,
faith" (Smith 1977: 69), that it is able to function
therapeutically for the dying person. In their shared
emphasis on the cruciality of this existential dynamic,
Smith and Kubler-Ross are in agreement in their
understanding of faith. But there is a difference, and
to its elucidation we now turn briefly.

Though Kubler-Ross emphasizes the engaged and
emotional aspects of positive, death-accepting,
religiousness ('integrity and intensity'), she still
seems to perceive this faith quality as a relation to
propositions. It is beliefs that comprise the focus of
one's concern and dedication; it is beliefs which are
sincerely held and internalized. The specific nature
of the beliefs seem inconsequential for, as we saw in

the initial questions and answer, the same quality of authenticity and commitment can exist in relation to quite different conceptions of the world and afterlife. What matters is not their content, but their existence as an object of sincere internalization.

In Smith's judgement, this contrasts sharply with the New Testament where only four percent of the pistis, pisteuo occurrences have a proposition as object. In the new Testament the overwhelming majority of instances have a thing, or a person, as object (especially Christ and God), or have no object (Smith 1977: 72). It has to be borne in mind that even where the object of faith is propositional, the relation is not one of believing it, (in the modern sense) but rather recognizing its patent truth and then committing oneself to living in terms of its factuality.

In delineating the object of faith in terms of what historically is only a minor ingredient of religious faith, namely ideas, Kubler-Ross exaggerates their importance and stands in contrast with Smith. Moreover, by failing to see that certain ideas, sincerely internalized, would lead not to acceptance but to despair, she paradoxically minimizes their role. For different concepts are susceptible to the same existential interpretation, or may function in a therapeutically similar way, only within limits. It is obvious that certain ideas -- if sincerely internalized and lived out with integrity -- would lead to calamitous consequences.

In summary, and at the risk of oversimplifying, it may be said that both Kubler-Ross and Smith see (modern) believing as comprised of two basic elements: (1) ideas and (2) tentativeness. But whereas Kubler-Ross finds transformational faith in the replacement of tentativeness by whole-hearted commitment, retaining the ideational element as the object of committed internalization, Smith perceives faith not only as the substitution of a provisional attitude by certitude, but also (usually) as the abandonment of the propositional element as the focus of faith.

4. Transcendent Commitment (Faith) in Mwalimu Imara

Rather than pursuing Smith's conception of faith as the crucial religious quality, I shall elaborate the role of faith by turning to a useful article by Mwalimu

Imara, "Dying as the Last Stage of Growth." Imara, relying heavily on Tillich and Haratounian for his theological inspiration, has given an interesting and for the most part cogent depiction of this faith quality which is other than belief and which facilitates dying well. I have schematized the description a little differently than Imara and amplified it somewhat, but (with reservations to be noted) I am largely in agreement with his interpretation.

(1) Faith for Imara is in the first place, a quality of <u>commitment</u>, i.e., single minded dedication of the whole self to what is experienced, or decided upon, as supremely valuable. It is a quality of integration of all personal facets and all motivations, needs and purposes.

(2) Secondly, faith entails a specific commitment to ultimate soteriological <u>transformation</u>. Those who possess this quality are characterized by constant growth and expansion, by a conative urgency to bring the empirical self into line with the ideal vision of the self. It is a thrust to transcend the limited and broken self, though without ending in utopianism and perfectionism.

(3) In the third place, faith involves a commitment to authenticity, to genuine experience. It is commitment to knowing oneself in the sense of becoming <u>aware</u> of what one truly is in the struggle for self-transcendence. It is the abolition of conventional roles in the quest for 'original experience'.

(4) Fourthly, faith entails commitment to other persons in trusting and caring <u>love.</u> It is opening oneself to the needs of others -- listening to them -- and opening oneself to be cared for and helped by others.

(5) The quality of life that makes acceptance of death possible includes, in the fifth place, commitment to some "operational blueprint or life script we refer to in order to determine our next steps in life and to make sense of the last few". (158)

Without such a <u>coherent world view</u> within which one's life finds a place and a meaning, the prospect is aimlessness and emptiness. Ultimately, without such a cosmology, one knows neither who one truly is, nor what should be supremely valued. There is, accordingly, a certain artificiality in Imara's discrimination of the conditions of fulfilled, transcendent living (for our purpose we may say simply, "faith") as first, self-identity, second, mutual inter-personal communication, and third, a coherent, directional world-view. The answer to the first question -- "Who am I?" -- is implied in the answer to the second and third question, namely; "To whom do I commit myself?" and "How do I go about living my commitment?" I come to know who I am as I understand what it is to which I commit myself, whether that be other persons, or a world-view, or both.

The most critical reservation about Imara's scheme, however, concerns a possible regression to the ideational, or 'belief', understanding of personal faith and to this problem we must devote somewhat more attention. Such a conceptual construction would contradict the primary thrust of my argument and would, indeed, contravene Imara's own highly existential understanding of faith. Imara betrays a certain uneasiness with this philosophical ingredient of faith. He cautions that, "This cosmological understanding need not be articulated in any systematic way, or even be entirely conscious, but it must express itself as a dominant integrating pattern in our life." (158). Further, "Our understanding, conscious or not, must make sense of our behaviour and the behaviour of others." (158).

This problem of unconscious understanding, of theoretically unformulated world-views, is a difficult one. It is true that ontological presuppositions about human nature, history, physical nature, and God, are frequently implicit in the myths and symbols to which religious communicants devoutly adhere without ever moving to a conceptual formulation or systematic and coherent arrangement of them. Such a cosmology could be said to be presupposed in the sense that it is not brought to intellectual consciousness. But then it becomes difficult to grasp how Imara can exhort his readers to adopt -- as a condition of faith, of creative and transcendent life -- such a meaning-conveying world-view. Only if the cosmology is a self-conscious conceptual framework for one's valuing and acting, can it be enjoined. The attendant faith, however, would then be a matter of ideas, to which, admittedly, one is urged to be fully and truly committed.

The problem is exacerbated when we take note of the high degree of cosmological relativism in Imara's thought. He tells us that, "Each of us has our special way of looking at the world" (158), suggesting that one way is as good as another provided it is taken as a global framework within which our life finds meaning and value. This same sort of relativism is echoed by Kubler-Ross when she asserts that the spirit is eternal and instructs her readers to "interpret this in any way that makes you comfortable".

We are faced with the same paradox that was adumbrated earlier when we examined the role of beliefs in Kubler-Ross' understanding of authentic religiousness. On the one hand, faith is still viewed in a excessively conceptual way. Although there is some ambivalence on this matter, the suggestion is strong that faith entails the adoption of a worldview construed as a conceptual system interpreting the world and our place in it, which one can voluntarily decide to embrace. On the other hand, the role of beliefs is minimized by the suggestion that the specific content of a belief system is irrelevant for faith, the only significant factor being the subjective experience of a cosmology that supplies orientation to the possessor. This assessment contradicts the evidence that different, particular ideas can be internalized in such a way that they do become specific formative forces in personality. Imara is, nevertheless, moving in the right direction when he affirms the necessity for faith of an ultimate set of perspectives, attitudes and values that are implicitly (or sometimes explicitly) taken to be appropriate reflections of the world as it really is, and which, in turn, animate one's judgements, responses, and deeds.

A further allusion to Smith's view of faith, that confirms much of what has been said about Imara, might well be inserted here. Perhaps the most penetrating insight that Smith contributes to our understanding of religiousness and death is the perception that in a majority of cases in the New Testament faith appears without an object. He insists, furthermore, that it is peremptory to declare that the object -- Christ or the Kerygma -- is understood when the authors do not say so.

Rather, Smith proposes that faith (though it may

- 150 -

also have an object), is to be understood as a generic human quality, the possession of which distinguishes persons one from another. Those who do not have the virtue of faith are characterized instead by the property of nihilism. Just as there may be the generic quality of love (as in 1 Cor. 13), or anxiety, without a specified object, similarily there is the generic quality of faith.

Faith is characterized by a cluster of attitudes and valuations: faith is confidence and trust, it is integration of the person, wholeness, serenity and courage, a sense of at-homeness in the Universe, possession of meaning in the world and one's own life (which explains in part why an atheist may have the ability to reach acceptance of death), faith is self-forgetting charity towards others (93).

5. Conclusion

The works of Smith and Kubler-Ross, though stemming from highly diverse starting points, provide a fruitful juxtaposition.

Kubler-Ross' clinical findings may be seen as confirming Smith's theory that there has been a radical shift in religious consciousness from an almost unreflected recognition of transcendent truth and commitment to it, to an epistemologically sceptical and existentially tentative frame of mind. Kubler-Ross and her associates have discovered that being religious can create a type of personality for whom death is deprived of terror; but they also detected that this was religiousness of a special sort. More precisely, religiousness that was comprised of 'believing' was especially abortive. Believing -- adhering to propositions in a half-hearted way -- simply did not induce acceptance and serenity in the face of death. However, religiousness which consisted of 'having faith', that is, consisted of a quality of commitment, self-transcendence, honest self-awareness, mutual love and communication, and cosmic meaning, was able to transform despair of death into creative human growth.

Approaching from the other side, it may be said that Smith provides a theoretical and historical analysis that explains why the believing mode of religiousness should be, as Kubler-Ross found, ineffective. For believing -- unlike faith which relates the devotee to transcendent truth in transformative commitment -- entails perplexity as to cosmic truth and hesitancy about self-involvement. In the crisis of dying, these dispositions of believing prove to be sterile. The next chapter will serve to enlarge our understanding of faith which transcends death. Our focus will be fixed especially on the love dimension of personal faith.

NOTES

1. All of the questions and answers that follow are taken from Elizabeth Kubler-Ross, Questions and Answers on Death and Dying.

REFERENCES

Imara, Mwalimu
1975 "Dying as the Last Stage of Growth" in Elizabeth Kubler-Ross ed., Death: The Final Stage of Growth. Englewood Cliffs, New Jersey: Prentice-Hall.

Kubler-Ross, Elizabeth
1974 Questions and Answers on Death and Dying. New York: Collier Books.

Smith, Wilfred Cantwell
1977 Belief and History. Charlottesville: University Press of Virginia.

CHAPTER TEN

THE AXIOLOGICAL PRESENCE OF DEATH IN LIFE

One of the dominant, but so far muted, purposes in writing this book may be attained by clarifying the meaning of the phrase "axiological presence of death". The phrase itself is Karl Rahner's, the prominent Roman Catholic theologian. It is a cumbersome phrase, admittedly, but I have found it useful in default of formulating a satisfactory alternative. Let us try to unpack what that phrase means.

To begin with, the word 'axiological' means pertaining to value. Literally it is the 'logos' or rational analysis of values, this latter meaning being contained in the 'axio' part of that phrase (from the Greek axon, meaning axle). Consequently, the axiological presence of death must have something to do with either the value of death itself or with death generated values, or both.

1. Death as Psychological Event

The first thing to notice is that the axiological presence of death clearly implies a contrast with another kind of death, specifically, the biological presence of death. The axiological presence of death expresses the conviction that even when biological extinction has not yet taken place, death can be present in an anticipatory way. Before biological death occurs, the meaning and impact of death may be already present as a psychological or 'spiritual' event. Before the heart stops beating and the electrical activity of the brain ceases, death may be experienced as a prospect and as a formative power. This anticipation and influence of death may be termed the proleptic experience of death, 'proleptic' being understood as a future event making its impact felt in the present. Just as the eschatological consummation of the world might be part of the consciousness of the believer proleptically, that is, in advance of the end of the world, even so, one's death in the future may be experienced in the present life. Instead of the axiological presence of death, we could talk of the proleptic presence of death, but we would lose the stress on values. The phrase 'axiological presence of death' is a plea to recognize both death's contemporary presence to the imagination and death's value-creating, power even during life.

This view of the difference between biological death and axiological death should be distinguished from other views that also postulate the presence of death in life. Paul Tillich made a distinction between the forces of life and death, both constantly present in the life of the subject. There is a dialectical rhythm in every person's life between organic life and cellular destruction. Life is made up of this oscillation between birth and decay, life and death. But this cellular destruction as an ongoing process is not what I mean when I speak of the presence of death in life. It is misleading to assimilate ongoing cellular decay to that final biological annihilation which is what we normally mean by death. Tillich's affirmation that death is always present in life is nothing more than a biological statement that there is at all points physical decay as well as cellular repair in the organism. When I refer to the axiological presence of death, I intend to signify the meaning and value of death held in the present by the living subject.

Another interpretation of the presence of death during life is that given by Mwalimu Imara to whom I made reference when analyzing the distinction between faith and belief in meeting death. In his article "Dying as the Last Stage of Growth", Imara draws a series of analogies between the changes that are an ongoing characteristic of life, and biological death. There are changes of career, of relationship, of belief and value systems, and so on. All of these changes, Imara claims, can be construed as a kind of death. Whenever there is a radical break with the preceding pattern of life and a new risky undertaking, there is a kind of death which is necessary in order to grow. Imara illustrates this with episodes from his own life; he refers to the transformations in his career from businessman printer to seven year university student while he took a Divinity degree, followed by a career as a minister, and subsequently as a pastoral counsellor, particularly with the dying. Each one of these transformations or life stages can be considered a death. Such changes involve dying to old ways of life in order to attain new meanings and relationships.

That is, I believe, a highly vulnerable analogy. It is a mistake to homologize these life changes, risky

- 156 -

as some may be, with the awesome finality of biological extinction. Imara's affirmation of the presence of death in life, which assumes death to be similar to the painful adjustments that take place when we are obliged to abandon an old self, an old value system, or an old accustomed pattern for something new, is not the kind of presence that I have in mind. It is seriously misleading to equate the singular finality of bodily destruction with a change in mate or a change in employment. Death entails a qualitatively different event and experience. To assimilate risk-taking, adjustment and growth in life to the dreadful and terminal change of death discloses one's failure to really grasp the meaning of death. When I speak of the axiological presence of death I mean something quite other than a weak similarity between life-changes and the final rupture which alone should truly be spoken of as death.

In death, that which has threatened us all our life, namely, loss of intimate relation and hence loss of personal meaning and value, is confronted with seeming unconditional power and finality. Though there is a continuity between the existential threats during life and those of death, there is also a qualitative difference which greatly exacerbates the anxiety of death. The qualitative difference lies in the absence of hope that broken relation, lovelessness, can be rectified in the future -- a hope which is possible in the despair of life, but seems impossible in our dying.

William May, in his article "The Sacral Presence of Death in Contemporary Society", gives a good statement of the contrast between biological and proleptic, psychological death. He says, "Death is not merely a biological incident that ends human life. It reaches into the course of life, gripping the human heart with love, fear, hope, worry, and flight, long before the end is reached" (May 1969: 171).

2. Death Itself as Value or Disvalue

The second point that derives from the phrase 'axiological presence of death' is that death may be experienced and interpreted positively as value or negatively as disvalue. I need not belabour this point because throughout this discussion the romanticization of death has been resisted. Though competing views have been acknowledged, the dominant view has been that ordinarily death is felt as a negative value, as a destructive quality. The reasons have been enumerated on various occasions: death threatens the cessation of creative work, the end of personal identity as we normally know it, and separation from loved ones -- the point at which death's power manifests itself most painfully. The axiological presence of death means that in advance of our dying we can make a judgement about the worth or unworth of death. My conclusion, exposited at length, is a negative judgement: death is experienced as disvalue. One way in which death is present psychologically before biological extinction is, accordingly, as anxiety, with its overtones of dread and bafflement.

Acceptance of this conclusion, however, obliges us to acknowledge and deal with a reservation. Does anxiety about death necessarily always imply a negative valuation of death? Is it possible to hold that anxiety is good? At face value, this is an untenable position in that religious traditions, we have contended, come into being as an attempt to deliver persons from such existential anxieties. However, in an instrumental or secondary sense, it might be argued that anxiety has a beneficial effect in that it leads to certain positive values by way of reaction. In a straightforward sense, though, death-anxiety evokes a negative valuation of death; so much so that these two ways of pointing to the initial experience of death -- anxiety and negativity -- are, in fact, synonomous.

3. Death as Generator of Value

The sense of the phrase 'axiological presence of death' which comes closest to its heart emphasizes the role of death (or, to speak more precisely, the consciousness of death) in discovering and inspiring commitment to significant values. James Laney expresses this point well:

> Death in this view is no longer only value-negation. Rather, the anticipation of that final negation as far as historic life is concerned serves to provide the basis for value-affirmation, for a deepened sense of time's unique preciousness and the singular opportunity. (Laney 1969: 235).

In consequence of death's inevitability and apparent finality, there emerges a summons to make this life and its precarious time-span count for the most. What Laney called the temporality and singularity of life induces a strong sense of moral consciousness and seriousness. In a way the point is a very simple one and does not need to be dressed up in such elaborate language. Basically the point is that if you know you are going to die, the chances are you will devote yourself to what you judge to be worthwhile. You will strive to avoid wasting time and energy on those goals and projects which assume low priority relative to the highest that is open to human beings.

Let me cite Laney again: "Death sets the unavoidable limitation upon life's 'time' in such a way as to invest it with utter singularity" (234-5). I take 'singularity' to mean that because of death's apparent finality, and certainly because of its inevitability, the life span of any particular person provides a unique opportunity to make those choices which will make his or her life count. The very nature of temporality as fundamental constitutent of life evokes an urgency to live it well. Temporality means simply the sense that life is qualified by a time limit. This sense of temporality drives us to wrest meaning and worth from life while opportunities still are available to us to do so. Laney goes on to say, "The awareness of death colours all decisions in life and freights them with moral seriousness" (235). Further: "Time's movement towards death not only requires a concentration upon the one choice among the many, it also bespeaks the irrevocable nature of that choice and thus of life itself" (235). Time's movement towards death -- the temporality of human life -- impels us to discern, among the range of choices open to us, which ones really deserve priority; it concentrates our attention on the pursuit of those values while opportunity exists.

Death, it is evident, has an impact on our ethical decisions. The proleptic experience of death not only precipitates an assessment upon death itself as value or disvalue; it also serves as a powerful incentive to attend to the highest goals and values.

4. The Denial Versus the Axiological Presence of Death

Attention has been drawn to Ernest Becker's thesis in The Denial of Death that the fundamental repression in life is not the repression of sex but the repression or denial of mortality. This reinterpretation generates a paradox that that which is necessary for a fulfilling life also seems to go against the grain of life. On the one hand, we need to experience -- axiologically -- the value-creating effect of death in order to live well, positively and creatively. On the other hand, the anticipation of death is frightful and, therefore, instinctively evaded. If it is true that people inherently deny death, (reinforced, at times by cultural forces such as those in the contemporary world which encourage the denial of death) then it is important that there should be cultural institutions like religious traditions to induce people to do that which by nature they do not want to do, namely, face their death. Religious traditions point people away from the way they naturally perceive the world and away from their natural inclinations, to the real, sacred world and a commensurate way of living.

This is very clear in the Buddha's case. In his analysis, life is suffering. But people do not really know that; they are intent on accumulating as much pleasure as they can. They think pleasure is possible and desirable, and they set themselves resolutely to attain it. Consequently, the Buddha exhorts people to go against the psychic grain. People must be taught that the things they crave are really illusory -- at least in the sense that they ultimately bring no lasting satisfaction. Most people believe if only they could get that new house, or new car; if only they could win her love, or, conversely, get rid of his; if only they could have two children, one of each sex with straight teeth and high IQs; then life would be perfect or nearly so. The Buddha points out that though this is what most people think, it is not really so simple. Such persons must be disabused of their illusions and attain insight into reality, which means, as a starting point, recognizing the painful character of human life.

The transformation process is similar respecting death. The deep seated human reluctance to acknowledge mortality -- the thrust to deny or mask death in many clever ways -- must be countered. People instinctively decline to face their death. Accordingly, religious traditions seek to unmask these deceptions and force people to appropriate death axiologically. Those who seek salvation and truth must be under no illusions about their mortality, finitude, and temporality. The recognition of the finite amount of time at human disposal should incline us to seek those things which have highest and abiding worth.

In order to avoid confronting their death, humans repress their anxiety about death. But the human reluctance to face death exists against the background of the impossibility of ultimately evading the awareness of death. This is because there are levels of consciousness that keep reminding us of our repressed mortality. Mediaeval sages kept a human skull on their desk to remind them of their mortality. We do not, however, need a skull on our desks because there are forces of consciousness that nag us with intimations of mortality. Nor is that just a characteristic of old people. Kastenbaum, one of the early thanotologists, did a study of young people and found that even they are uneasy about their mortality, about the fragility of their existence.

A personal note might illustrate this point. One spring, at the height of the run-off of winter snows, a small group of us shot a set of rapids in our canoes about a half dozen times. I was intrigued that our sixteen year old son, whom I regarded as a white-water enthusiast because he had done a fair amount of kayaking in Vermont, was apprehensive. He was the first one to go through with an adult historian. I thought he would be exuberant after his successful run. Instead he subtly conveyed the impression that he would be just as happy to quit at that point. I noted this and asked, "Mark, what's the matter." I added "Are you frightened?" I said it kindly, not as a macho father, berating his son. To tell the truth, I was frightened myself, but I wanted to understand the psychology of his anxiety. I expected to be apprehensive; I didn't expect him to be. Robert Kastenbaum (1965) has got it dead right (if the pun be permitted) when he observes that even amongst young people there is apprehension about death. Mark had read in the newspaper just the preceding week that a canoe had dumped in these very same rapids and that one of the canoeists had trouble getting out of the cold water. One cannot stay long in that freezing spring run-off; canoeists have died in the pursuit of exhilarating sport. Following a capsize the intense water pressure can pin a bobbing paddler in a weir effect preventing an exit from the frigid flow.

There is a scarey element about white water paddling and Mark knew it. Even amongst the young there is an apprehensive sense of the vulnerability, not only of their own lives but also of the lives of those who are responsible for them, mainly, of course, their mothers and fathers.

There is reluctance to acquiesce in one's mortality, but this reluctance co-exists with the conscious or unconscious knowledge that death is a distressing reality. Religious traditions (and certain existentialist and secular traditions as well) are saying, in effect: "Stop the repression. Let those levels of consciousness that are warning you about mortality and limitation speak. When you let them speak you experience death as present reality. Then there would be at least a strong inclination to live by higher values."

In order to differentiate the presence of death-in-life in its value creating function, from the presence of death-in-life in its manifestations as anxiety and evasion, I prefer to use the term 'proleptic' in a wide sense to cover all forms of death's contemporary impact including its effects of dread and denial, and to restrict the term 'axiological' to that internalization of death's meaning that results in the generation of positive, life-enhancing values.[1]

We may summarize this part of the argument by reiterating that death is proleptically present in life, exercising an impact and power upon human existence, in three modes. First, as existential anxiety -- as source of universal dread and perplexity. Since this is so painful a condition, this awareness of death is commonly repressed. Consequently, in the second place, death-anxiety is present in repressed, sublimated or pornographic forms. The third way in which death is present is axiologically. Whereas existential anxiety is universal and inevitable, axiological presence is a condition deliberately sought and attained by some. Axiological presence means that death, normally experienced as disvalue, paradoxically achieves a certain positive valuation in the light of its capacity to generate commitment to supreme value.

Death will not likely function as a catalyst for human pursuit of positive value, unless denial is overcome and death's character as dread and perplexity is acknowledged. It is because death threatens life at its highest spiritual or symbolic level that it is able to inspire an intention to attain life's highest possibilities, before death forecloses this aim.

5. Axiological Re-Interpretions of Religions

This axiological way of interpreting death may illumine some religious messages in other than the conventional ways. The resurrection, both of Jesus and of his disciples in the last days, could be understood not as the eschatological reversal of the human tragedy of death characterized by pain and separation, but as an interpretation of the _meaning_ of death. The resurrection points to the transformative possibilities made available by death. By accepting one's mortality and experiencing "the axiological presence of death in life", one has the impetus to appropriate resurrection life, that is, to live creatively, committedly yet serenely, in the light of life's highest values.

A further instance of religious reinterpretation in the light of the insight into death as axiologically present, may be found in primitive religiousness. In our introduction to the interpretation of death as existential anxiety, we observed that in primitive societies, according to Eliade, death is experienced as anguish, an ordeal which is, however, transmuted by the conviction that it is also a rite of passage to another -- potentially at least -- superior existence. The same interpretation of the anxiety of death as necessary but transitory ordeal, preliminary to a blessed deliverance, is found in Hindu faith. "To the non-Europeans, Death is neither definitive nor absurd; on the contrary, the anxiety aroused by the imminence of death is already a promise of resurrection, reveals the presentiment of re-birth into another mode of being, and this is a mode which transcends Death." (Eliade 1967: 243)

Presumably, the myths which portray this passage to a new mode of being are understood literally as well as existentially by their original audience. But how can death be experienced as initiation and passage for those of secularized consciousness who are incapable of believing the literal construction of myths of afterlife?

The answer may be found in understanding one's

- 163 -

physical death, proleptically experienced, as catalyst for one's mystological or spiritual death and rebirth. Such proleptic or anticipatory death in the form of anxiety, rather than actual physical death, becomes itself the initiatory ordeal which issues in a new mode of being in the world. This new mode -- lived in the awareness of one's finitude and mortality -- is characterized by a heightened dedication to higher values and by appropriation of superior life qualities. To express the same point somewhat differently: one's death (or rather the internalized anxiety of one's physical death) can be metamorphisized into axiological death from which one is resurrected or transformed into a new being, living a life transcending previous illusions and banal or destructive practice.

It should be further noted that in the interaction between the anxiety of death and the religious therapeutic answer, the pain and perplexity of death may not be totally obliterated. Even for those who take more or less literally the messages of 'afterlife' conveyed in their traditions, there may be an ongoing dialectic between the anxiety of death and the blessedness of the afterlife, until the final vanquishing of death in the forms portrayed in various myths. There is, it might be said, an ongoing rite of passage which is completed only at the point of actual death and insertion into the afterlife, however conceived. Ordeal (in the form of anxiety), and transformation (in the form of afterlife proleptically experienced), may well co-exist in the earthly psychic life.[2]

6. The Ultimate Value That Transcends Death

Killinger (1969), writing on death in contemporary literature, corroborates much of the foregoing. He says that contemporary literature attests that death becomes the act of compression, packing life with sensibility, meaning and values. But one is entitled to ask: which values? It is difficult to say precisely what positive life-values are implicit in the axiological presence of death. There are, however, hints given here and there, even within the limited resources of this enquiry, that the axiological presence of death does point towards a specific value. It is, to put it straightforwardly, the value of love. To illustrate with an episode treated by Killinger: In Beckett's one act play Krapp's Last Tape we have the

scene of Krapp playing his tape recorder over and over
again. Over the years he has recorded his impressions
and he now backs up the tape and records his
impressions of impressions. This goes on year after
year as he sits there in a kind of tedious and mindless
repetition of his tape recordings. But one event seems
to crystalize him into attentiveness and
responsiveness. One event seems to be meaningful to
him. This is an experience with a girl in a canoe. No
details are given, but we are entitled to extrapolate
that though everything else in Krapp's repetitive
catalogue is boring and empty and meaningless, the
experience of the girl in the canoe stands out as an
episode of meaning. As the tape of life is winding
out, Krapp discerns that what really counted, and
really should count, is intimate relation with one
another.

In "The Death of Ivan Ilych", there are the same
intimations. When he lies dying, the things that the
perspective of death now discloses as significant are
not what he had previously thought; they are not his
great successes, not the professional goals attained,
not criminals judged nor innocent people vindicated,
not the important people known and cultivated and
socialized with. What is now significant are the
seemingly trivial and inconsequential things; to wit:
a striped soccer ball, the smell of whose leather used
to please him, the caresses of his nanny; the smell of
his mother's hair, a few random experiences of love
with women before he became obsessed with career
ambition. In effect, the value that is vindicated in
the perspective of death, is the value of relational
intimacy and love.

Corroboration of this conclusion may be found in
one interpretation of the Genesis creation and fall
narrative. In the course of exegeting Genesis 3:3, the
Interpreter's Bible declares that "there is no
suggestion in vs. 19 ... that man's return to the
ground was a consequence of his disobedience; the
implication is rather that this was his natural end."
In order words, the traditional view that death is a
punishment for sin, does not stand up.

The exegesis goes on to say: "The inference would
seem to be unavoidable that for J [the Yahwist strand
of narration] not death itself but man's attitude
toward death as the final frustration of a frustrated
life was the last consequence of the alienation from
God which his rebellion had caused." Not death, but

the dread of death is the punishment for sin.

This theme is picked up in the exegesis of 3:19 itself (including the phrase , 'you are dust, and to dust you shall return'). Here the point is made that the emergence of death anxiety is the consequence of estrangement, both from the creator and from the human community. It is sin -- the attempt to arrogate to the human ego absolute powers of domination over others -- that generates the fear of death. "Man's disordered relationship and his fear of death are inextricably bound up together, the consequence of his alienation from God".

I believe this analysis of the etiology of death-anxiety is correct in important respects; in chapter two I argued that one of the major constituents of the dread of death is the rupture of human relation. It is true, that I incline towards a demythologized or secular interpretation which stresses the separation from human community rather than from an objectified supreme being. In any case, an important inference follows: the restoration of relation allays the anxiety of death. Just as there is a degree of continuity between the hurt of alienation during life and the anxiety of seemingly irreversible alienation at death, there is also a connection between the healing resolution attainable in life and that possible at death. Loneliness and estrangement can be transformed during life into communion and reconciliation. A love that heals the despair of separation is possible. The testimony of some of the dying is that the attainment of such love also makes dying with relative acceptance possible.

There is a paradox here. We noted that it is especially the prospect of the truncation of human relation that invests death with its capacity to evoke fear. At the same time, it is claimed that the attainment of love deprives death of its despair. How is this paradox to be understood?

It seems that the attainment of love -- even if it should come late at the time of one's dying as it did for Ivan Ilych -- bestows value on an individual's life because one feels to have achieved the supremely worthwhile value of life, namely, the bequeathal and reception of self-giving care. The knowledge that one loves and receives love carries with it the conviction that brief and risky as is the human pilgrimage on earth, it has, notwithstanding, attained the pearl of great price. To achieve life's highest value, defined as that profound and sacrificial sharing of life and destiny which is love, is to have truly lived in defiance of death. One can die well because one knows one has not failed, has not been cheated of the highest gift life has to offer.

In effect, we go full circle, or if one prefers a different spatial image, we oscillate between life and death. Death becomes acceptable, its destructive anxiety mitigated, if not eradicated, by living according to the supreme value of love. But, paradoxically, life can be lived lovingly and well only if it is lived in the knowledge of our death, made painful by our bonds of love whose termination we fear. The axiological presence of death generates that single-pointedness that allows us to see clearly, first, what matters and, second, the cruciality of the time in which what matters must be possessed.

The following brief passage of Herman Feifel (1960: 70) suggests both directions or polarities:

A man's birth is an uncontrollable event in his life, but the manner of his departure from life bears a definite relation to his philosophy of life and death. We are mistaken in considering death a purely biologic event. Life is not comprehended truly or lived fully unless the idea of death is grappled with honesty.

Life of a certain quality (on the present thesis this means a loving life) generates a victorious relation to death; death generates the mood and motive for living that love.

1. In this positive interpretation of the axiological presence of death, I am at odds with Laney who says:

> It needs to be acknowledged frankly, however, that this "axiological" presence of death throughout life does not necessarily insure a constructive attitude and response. In the absence of hope and without constructive faith transcending our temporal end, the presence of death in life can lead to a clutching at value, to an "ethics of death."(Laney 1969: 236)

Laney's neutral interpretation, however, appears to contradict the main thrust of his exposition of this concept, an exposition which serves to affirm the value-creating power of the psychological internalization of one's death. But definitions are rarely worth fighting over so long as they are clearly specified and consistently applied.

2. This may be the appropriate place to register a caveat about Kubler-Ross' theory of acceptance of death which has almost assumed the status of a normative dogma. As a corrective, one should place alongside the important idea of accepting one's death, Camus' contrary counsel in The Myth of Sisyphus that it is "essential to die unreconciled and not of one's own free will". It is likely that in the dialectical interplay between acceptance and rebellion the most authentic attitude towards death will emerge for most people.

REFERENCES

Eliade, Mircea
  1967 Myths, Dreams and Mysteries: The Encounter between Contemporary Faiths and Archaic Realities. New York: Harper Torch books.

Feifel, Herman
    1960 "Death: Relevant Variable in Psychology" in
        Rollo May, ed., <u>Existential Psychology</u>. New
        York: Harper and Row.

Kastenbaum, Robert
    1965 "Time and Death in Adolescence" in Herman
        Feifel, ed., <u>The Meaning of Death</u>. New York:
        McGraw Hill.

Killinger, John
    1969 "Death and Transcendence in Contemporary
        Literature" in Liston O. Mills, ed.,
        <u>Perspectives on Death</u>. Nashville: Abingdon.

Laney, James T.
    1969 "Ethics and Death" in Liston O. Mills, ed.,
        <u>Perspectives on Death</u>. Nashville: Abingdon.

May, William
    1969 "The Sacral Power of Death in Contemporary
        Experience" in Liston O. Mills, ed.,
        <u>Perspectives on Death</u>. Nashville: Abingdon.

AFTERWORD

As originally planned, this book was to end with a chapter entitled "The Structure of Religious Coping Strategies". This was to be a phenomenological analysis intended to uncover and present the universal forms manifest in the multiplicity and diversity of religious teachings on the meaning of death and 'afterlife', this latter term being construed in a wide sense as transformative antidotes to death.

I believe a reasonable case has been made that beneath the diversity of religious images, stories, doctrines, and rituals pertaining to death, one may discern a common structure of anxiety, of dread and bafflement in the face of death that calls forth a transformative or therapeutic answer in the symbols of religions.

But the common structure of religious coping strategies (if, indeed, there be one), does not come so readily to the surface. We have seen that there exists a high degree of diversity in views of afterlife. Though the Christian tradition, as it unfolded in history, did effect a synthesis (of sorts) of the doctrines of immortality of the soul and resurrection of the body, scholars like Oscar Cullman have disputed its normative legitimacy. Such integration, Cullman argued, masks the radical divergence of two ways of perceiving reality: one the biblical, the other Hellenistic. Even if Cullman has overstated the degree of opposition between the Hebraic and Christian vision of resurrection of the body, and the Hellenistic vision of the immortal soul, it is nonetheless evident that the various coping doctrines we have examined are difficult to reconcile.

Reynolds and Waugh (1977) attempt a concise phenomenology of death under the general categories of 'Disjunction', 'Continuity', 'Transition', 'Integration' and 'Transformation'. The forms of consciousness represented by these terms have been discussed, in the same or different language, in this present study. Clearly, I find that Reynolds and Waugh have supplied useful interpretive concepts. However, most of them pertain to the meaning of death rather than the meaning of afterlife, which is my present concern. Moreover, these categories remain on a high level of generality which encompasses a great deal of diversity within the logical form.

What requires attention is the determination of forms of consciousness in the human encounter with death that can be formulated with more specific meaning. Is it possible to discover or abstract common features or structures of the different religious ideas of afterlife? Can we lay hold of a shared understanding of death and its transcendence that is implicit in all or most of the particular historical manifestations of concern with the pain and problem of death?

John Hick concludes his comparative study of death and eternal life with two proposals for a shared essence of the religious traditions of east and west. (His own term for this is "a global theology of death.") This common perspective is to be found not in all strands of religious traditions but principally in a qualified theism of biblical-type religions and in the _vishishtadvaita_ (qualified non-dualism) of Hinduism. The first universal theme is the discovery of the atman defined by Hick as "the complex collective consciousness of humanity" (461) or "the complex personal unity of mankind" (462). The second is the realization of union between the atman or collective human self and Ultimate Reality (God, Brahman, the Unconditioned, the Absolute, the Eternal).

The first feature, according to Hick, of all major religions -- the elimination of egoity in 'a perfect community of personal relationship' -- is probably compatible with my intimations of the death-transcending power of love. Describing such human relation Hick says, "The sense of our ultimate belonging together in total community is the unselfish love which the New Testament calls _agape_." (464)

However, Hick's search for a universal structure of seemingly diverse religious responses to death moves in a more metaphysical direction than I am inclined to go when we turn to his second proposal. The eschatological goal of the atman is eternal relationship to Ultimate Reality. Lacking his assurance about the Ultimate construed in his spiritual terms, I prefer to remain, at least provisionally, on the level of a demythologizing or existential interpretation that discerns the common religious structure in shared perspectives on the nature of human existence, values, and temporal possibilities.

I have ventured the view that personal intimacy

and human love -- which, on some religious interpretations, is but an earthly mirror of divine love -- function as an effective riposte to the threat of death. Tolstoy, in his portrayal of Ivan Ilych's death-bed transformation, Cantwell Smith, in his historical analysis of faith, and Imara in his depiction of human mutuality in the lives of the dying, come together in support of the thesis that the human quality that transcends death's destructive challenge is the giving and receiving of love, that is, human presence, commitment, caring and sharing.

In discussing the roles of faith and belief in meeting death (chapter nine), we noted that efficacious faith may be analysed under the aspects of commitment, transformation, awareness, love, and cosmic coherence. I do not think we are confronted with a conceptual competition between faith and love as the generic human quality that triumphs over death. At the very least, love may be acknowledged as the most important of that cluster of elements that comprises faith. My own view is that the various aspects of faith may be reduced, for many persons, at least, to the fundamental quality of gracious love. This compression of faith to love takes place on the basis of the most general definition of faith, proposed at various times throughout this study, as commitment to whatever reality is experienced as supremely true and valuable. The reality that meets this criterion and evokes a transformative integrity of self is the experience of that gracious love that accepts, upholds, and bears all things in spite of one's imperfections and frailty .

The problematic that remains and which causes me to suspend this discussion on death and afterlife at this point, is whether it is possible to argue convincingly that this transformative and healing quality of human love is, in fact, implicit in the various images and messages of 'afterlife' that we have examined (and, of course, the many more which we have not).

I would like to believe it is, but cannot, at this time demonstrate it.

REFERENCES

Hick, John
  1980 <u>Death and Eternal Life</u>. San Francisco: Harper & Row paperback edition. First published in 1976.

Reynolds, Frank and Waugh, Earle
  1977 <u>Religious Encounters with Death: Insights from The History and Anthropology of Religions</u>. University Park: The Pennsylvania State University Press.

Antonio R. Gualtieri is Professor of Religion, Carleton University, with special interests in problems of religious diversity, comparative religious ethics, and methodology. Previously, he served as a minister of The United Church of Canada and taught in the Religion Department at Vassar College.

Among the journals in which his articles have appeared are: SR Studies in Religion/Sciences Religieuses, Scottish Journal of Theology, Religious Studies, Journal for the Scientific Study of Religion, Theological Studies, Encounter, Religion and Society, Journal of Dharma, Journal of Ecumenical Studies, Canadian Ethnic Studies, Dalhousie Review. A book, Christianity and Native Traditions, dealing with missionary attitudes towards native religions in the Canadian Western Arctic, is in press.

Other interests include mountain trekking, canoeing, and skiing. He has been married to Margaret Nixon for twenty-nine years and they are the parents of three daughters and a son.